D1188008

PREHISTORY	Denise de Sonneville-Bordes, Ph. D.
ROME	Gilbert Picard, Professor at the Sorbonne, Paris
RUMANIA	Constantin Daicoviciu, Director of the Archaeological Institute of Cluj, and Emil Condurachi, Director of the Archaeological Institute of Bucarest
SOUTHERN CAUCASUS	Boris B. Piotrovsky, Director of the Hermitage Museum, Leningrad
SOUTHERN SIBERIA	Mikhail Gryaznov, Professor at the Archaeological Institute, Leningrad
SYRIA-PALESTINE I (Ancient Orient)	Jean Perrot, Head of the French Archaeological Mission in Israel
SYRIA-PALESTINE II (Classical Orient)	Michael Avi Yonah, Professor at the University of Jerusalem
THE TEUTONS	Rolf Hachmann, Professor at the University of Saarbrücken
TIBET	Giuseppe Tucci, President of the Italian Institute for the Middle and Far East, Rome
URARTU	Boris B. Piotrovsky, Director of the Hermitage Museum, Leningrad

ANCIENT CIVILIZATIONS

Series prepared under the direction of
Jean Marcadé, Professor of Archaeology
at the University of Bordeaux

JEAN-JACQUES HATT

CELTS AND GALLO-ROMANS

Translated from the French by James Hogarth

69 illustrations in colour; 150 illustrations in black and white

Barrie & Jenkins   London

© 1970 by NAGEL PUBLISHERS, GENEVA (SWITZERLAND)
First published in Great Britain
by Barrie & Jenkins
2 Clement's Inn, London WC2
Printed in Switzerland

CONTENTS

PREFACE

*T*he study of the "national antiquities", as they are called in France, has been given a quite new impetus in recent years. The archaeology of Gaul, for so long left to the unorganised, well-intentioned but sometimes unskilled efforts of local scholars, is now reaping full benefit from the improved excavation techniques and the emphasis on rigorous organisation and proper coordination which in every part of the world has marked the establishment of archaeology as a scientific discipline in the fullest sense of the term. It is no longer concerned merely to provide illustrative material for the traditional historians, but seeks to go back beyond the written sources or to supplement them by finding out things of which the ancient writers tell us nothing. For these sources, when they exist at all, are written in Latin or sometimes in Greek: their point of view is quite different from that of the Gauls themselves, and they approach the life of Gaul from the outside. And of course the essential problems are in fact concerned with the origins and the distinctive individuality of the indigenous peoples of Gaul, with their native genius and their gradual advance in refinement as a result of contacts with other cultures, their reactions to external influences and the way in which, despite romanisation, they retained their own personality and their ancestral beliefs.

Professor J. J. Hatt is himself deeply involved in the programme of archaeological research which is producing year by year a rapidly increasing store of carefully observed data and thus making it possible to suggest increasingly precise solutions to some of the outstanding problems. As director of the excavations at Le Pègue, a specialist in the historical stratigraphy of the Rhineland, an expert on Gallo-Roman sculpture and terra sigillata, *and the author of a recent very suggestive study of the Gundestrup cauldron and a penetrating analysis of the* interpretatio gallica *of mythological representations in Gaul, Professor Hatt is well qualified to contribute to the "Archaeologia Mundi" series this personal account of the problems, the methods and the results of the particular field of archaeology which he has made his own; and his account is at the same time a lucid and well informed survey of some of the central problems with which archaeologists are concerned at the present time.*

J. M.

11

INTRODUCTION

Archaeology has for too long been regarded as merely one of the auxiliary sciences of history. In fact, however, the leading part which it now plays in the study of ancient times and the increased resources it has drawn from physical and chemical techniques make it much more than the mere hand-maiden of the historians. In its present stage of development it is the very stuff of history, an advancing field of research (ἱστορία) which uses the new evidence it is daily wresting from the earth—the buildings, artifacts and material remains left by the various activities of men—to criticise, supplement and illuminate the few written documents which have survived from ancient times.

In our day archaeological science is being entirely renewed. It is steadily perfecting its own disciplines—the techniques of methodical excavation, of typological study, of cataloguing, of iconography, of comparison, analysis and interpretation—and can now look forward to enlisting the aid of the computer. It is making full use of auxiliary sciences like numismatics, the study of pottery, epigraphy and architecture. It is able to take advantage of modern techniques of physical and chemical analysis—radiography, spectrography, the study of remanent magnetism and residual radioactivity (carbon 14 dating). For the preliminary investigation of a site it can look to air photography and the measurement of the resistivity of the soil. In short, it is fully abreast of developments in the sciences concerned with the study of men's activities, which are no longer confined within the patterns of traditional scholarship—honourable though these are—but are constantly widening their horizons to encompass all the complexity of human civilisations and societies and seeking to improve their procedures so that they may the more effectively detect and interpret the evidence left by men's activities.

This renewal of archaeological method is accompanied by a fundamental change in historical perspective, which is particularly noticeable in relation to the peoples formerly regarded as backward and barbarian and to the provincial civilisations of the Roman Empire, on which we can glean so little precise information from the written sources.

This is particularly true of Gaul and its peoples, both before and after the Roman conquest. If we want fuller and more objective information than can be got from the written sources about their history and civilisation we must rely largely on the evidence produced by archaeology, which—particularly since the beginning of this century—has completely changed the historical perspective. This can readily be illustrated by a few examples.

13

The Greco-Latin historical tradition represents the Gauls as a brilliant and dynamic people, primitive and untutored, and capable of behaving on occasion like bloodthirsty savages. And it is certainly true that in the 4th and 3rd centuries before our era they overran Italy, surged into the Balkans and Greece, captured and sacked Rome, caused havoc throughout much of Europe, and extended their ravages as far as the sanctuary of Delphi. In this earlier period they played much the same part in Europe as did the Germanic tribes from the 3rd century A.D. onwards. Archaeology has shown, however, that as early as the 7th century B.C. the Gauls maintained regular trading relations with the countries bordering on the Mediterranean; that from the end of the 6th century they were profoundly marked by influences from Greece and Italy; and that they developed a civilisation of considerable complexity to which the peoples of the East—the Scythians and Iranians—also made their contribution. Instead of the rude and uncultured tribes described by the ancient authors, therefore, the evidence of archaeology, both past and present, introduces us to peoples who were fully in touch with economic and cultural influences emanating from the most civilised cities and nations of the period and had assimilated these imported elements and developed advanced techniques of craft production and a very individual and distinctive art of their own.

Coming to a later period—the Roman Empire—we should know little about the vast defensive works along the German frontier if we had to depend solely on one brief and slanted passage in Tacitus (*Germania*, XXIX, 4): "I am inclined not to reckon among the people of Germany the cultivators of the Agri Decumates, settled though they may be between Rhine and Danube. All the wastrels of Gaul, all the penniless adventurers seized on what was still no man's land. It was only later, when the frontier line of defence was drawn and the garrisons were moved forward, that they have become a sort of projection of the empire and a part of a province" (trans. H. Mattingly). The German excavations of the *Limes* and the archaeological exploration of the territory conquered by the Flavians after 70 A.D. have demonstrated the large-scale effort of pacification, fortification and settlement which produced such an efficiently organised frontier zone. This work has thrown light on an important chapter in the history of Rome and of Gaul; and recent discoveries in Alsace and Lorraine, following the stratigraphic investigations carried out during the past twenty years, have suggested an explanation for Tacitus's disparaging reference to the operations of the Flavian Emperors on the frontier between Gaul and Germany. The numerous traces of destruction which can be dated to the year 97 seem to indicate that at this period, during the reign of

Nerva, north-eastern Gaul was devastated by a large-scale military rising, which Tacitus may have seen as the consequence of an ill-considered policy of colonisation and conquest.

The humanist enthusiasm of the scholars of the 16th century delighted to recognise in the buildings of Gaul—the theatres and temples—the Roman models from which they were derived. Since then excavation and discovery, with proper archaeological recording, have shown that the temples built in the provinces were of a particular type, evidently based on native religious and liturgical traditions, and that the amphitheatres and theatres built in Gaul were likewise of distinctive form. The 18th century antiquaries were principally concerned to find in Gaul the reflection of Rome, of Greece, of the Orient. In our day, however, archaeology, having revealed over the years the distinctive characteristics of the civilisation of Gaul and the architecture and industry of the Roman province, seeks to define the very individual personality which was so strikingly displayed before the conquest and can be recognised in all the varied aspects of Gallo-Roman civilisation.

THE HISTORY OF ARCHAEOLOGICAL RESEARCH IN FRANCE

I

The Antiquaries

Whereas the Near Eastern excavations of the mid 19th century aroused wide public interest with their revelation of brilliant civilisations which had previously been entirely unknown, the exploration of Celtic and Roman Gaul has offered no comparable surprises. The archaeological discovery of Gaul has been the work of successive generations of enquirers who, from the 17th century to our own day, have sought to recover and interpret the remains of the past buried in its soil, gradually improving their techniques of research and adjusting their preconceived ideas in the light of the evidence they have laid bare.

The 17th Century

In the 17th century the people of France still preserved some memory of their origins, prompted by the Roman remains which were visible in much greater numbers then than they are now. The first scholarly studies of these remains appeared at this period. Characteristically, in an age concerned with the exact sciences and their practical applications, it was the roads, the aqueducts and the drains which first attracted the attention of scholars. Nicolas Bergier, author of a *History of the Highways of the Roman Empire*, wrote at the beginning of the century: "The greatness and the genius of Rome is manifested particularly in three fields—in its sewers, its aqueducts and its highways." Another scholar of the same period was Peiresc (1580–1637), who left important observations, drawings and notes on the antiquities of southern France and may be regarded as the ancestor and prototype of the "antiquaries" who were our first archaeologists.

The foundation of the Académie des Inscriptions et Belles Lettres (1679) gave particular impetus to the study of architecture and epigraphy. Colbert, Louis XIV's great minister, conceived the plan of recording and publishing all the Roman remains in France and commissioned the architect Mignard to prepare drawings and plans. In his *Researches on the Antiquities and Curiosities of the Town of Lyons* Spon produced one of our first collections of inscriptions, with commentaries which were a model of precise and positive interpretation.

The 18th Century

Valuable work was also done in the 18th century in compiling records of remains and inscriptions, notably by the Benedictines of the Congregations of Saint-Maur and Montfaucon. The contribution made by the monks of Montfaucon merits special mention. In the fifteen folio volumes of their great work, *Antiquity Explained and Represented in Figures* (1719), particular attention is devoted to the buildings, sculpture and inscriptions of Gaul; and this compilation is still a valuable source of reference, particularly as a record of remains which have since been destroyed.

Jean Daniel Schoepflin's *Alsatia Illustrata*, published in 1751, is an excellent regional study which provided a model and an example for others. A native of Baden, Schoepflin was appointed Professor of Eloquence and History at the University of Strasbourg in 1720 and devoted his life to studying the past of his adopted province. In this field he was a conscious innovator and can be regarded as one of the founders of the critical method in archaeology: "Ignoring all that had been written on antiquity by the chroniclers of the Middle Ages, he sought in antiquity itself the secrets which lay concealed in its mutilated remains, in the incomplete accounts to be found in its historians. Soon he was able to see Alsace in a new light: delving below the profound imprint left on its soil by the Romans, he recovered the traces of the inhabitants of an earlier day and was the first to reveal to his contemporaries the existence of the Celts." In this respect Schoepflin was a true pioneer and the real founder of the study of the national antiquities of France, which seeks to embrace the whole of Gallic and Gallo-Roman civilisation. About the same time, between 1752 and 1756, appeared the seven volumes of the *Collection of Egyptian, Greek, Etruscan, Roman and Gallic Antiquities* by the Comte de Caylus (1692–1765).

In the upsurge of revolutionary ideas at the end of the 18th century the national feeling of the French began to reach back to the remains of the remotest past. The term "national antiquities" appears for the first time in the title of a work published by Aubin-Louis Millin in 1790.

Even this brief survey is perhaps sufficient to show that French archaeology, in which there is such a remarkable revival of interest at the present time, can look back on a long tradition of valuable work which is still of interest, even though the older studies may not always be sufficiently precise and objective to be directly usable.

The Emergence of Modern Archaeology

In fact, though the excellent work done at the beginning of the 19th century by Arcisse de Caumont and the learned societies of the time must be acknowledged, modern archaeology in France goes no farther back than the middle of the 19th century. The following hundred years were a period of steady progress, during which successive generations of scholars developed and perfected their discipline into its present form.

What, it may be asked, were the additional elements required to transform the humanist learning of men like Schoepflin, Caylus and Caumont into an exact science of archaeology? First, perhaps, the realisation that the most insignificant vestiges of the past—the line of a ditch, a few post-holes, the remains of a hearth—are of interest to the historian and the archaeologist; and this in turn required the development of proper methods for excavating and recording remains of this kind. Secondly, the achievement of objectivity by ensuring the highest standards of precision in drawing and measurement, both in recording chance finds and the results of regular excavation and in the preparation of catalogues and reports; and this involved using all the new techniques developed by science in its continual advance. And finally in considering the wider perspectives and problems of archaeology it was necessary to build up a clear picture of the distinctive characteristics of Gallic history and civilisation, both before and after the Roman conquest, doing full justice not only to the basic indigenous elements but to the preservation of Gallic traditions after the conquest. It was necessary also to consider in more detail the developments peculiar to the area of Gallic culture resulting from its geographical situation, its political and economic history, and the varying patterns of external influences which converged on the area at different periods.

The Contribution of Napoleon III

The decisive advance began after 1850, as a result of a variety of circumstances. The Museum of National Antiquities at Saint-Germain-en-Laye was founded by Napoleon III in 1862, soon after the establishment of the Römisch-Germanisches Zentralmuseum in Mainz; and until the Franco-German war of 1870 the two museums maintained close contact with one another.

From 1860 onwards the Emperor caused systematic excavations to be carried out at Alesia, Gergovia and a number of other sites which had played a prominent part in Caesar's campaigns in Gaul, and was able to use the results in his *History of Julius Caesar*. These excavations, at first controlled by the Commission on the Topography of Gaul and later directed by Col. Stoffel, revealed remains of Roman entrenchments and works of military engineering, particularly at Alise-Sainte-Reine (Alesia). Where the original records have survived and it has been possible to check them the work seems to have been done conscientiously and objectively. If, as was said, "Caesar *(Plate 64)* was all the rage" with the Emperor and his entourage, his opponent Vercingetorix *(Plate 65)* soon became equally popular with those less devoted to the Emperor. From this period can be dated the propensity of the French to identify themselves with their Gallic ancestors, to detect in them some of their own traditional failings, and to surround the great battles of Caesar's campaigns with something of the glamour they have always built up round the great defeats of their history.

It was during this period, too, that the study of prehistory, founded by the Picard antiquary Boucher de Perthes, was beginning to evolve the methods which were to prove so fruitful when applied to historical archaeology. Later Edouard Lartet laid the foundations of a chronological classification of the Quaternary period, which Gabriel de Mortillet sought to extend to the whole of prehistory and proto-history (1880). Here Mortillet was following in the footsteps of Scandinavian scholars like Worsaae and Montelius, to whom most of the credit for laying down the broad lines of a classification of the protohistorical period is due. Montelius, a scholar of outstanding gifts, also established the methods of protohistorical study, laying solid foundations for an absolute chronology based on comparisons between the antiquities of western Europe and those of the countries round the Mediterranean, which were dated from the Bronze Age onwards by the historical records of Egypt and from a somewhat later period by those of the Middle Eastern countries.

The Excavation of the Limes

From 1890 onwards excavation of the Roman *Limes* in Germany was begun by the kingdom of Prussia, following the foundation of the Römisch-Germanische Kommission in Frankfurt, an offshoot of the Archaeological Institute of Berlin. The work was carried out on a larger scale and more systematically than the exploration by Napoleon III and Stoffel of Caesar's battlefields in Gaul; it is still in progress.

This work has yielded valuable results in many fields. In the first place—and this was its prime objective—it revealed a system of fortification which had hitherto been totally unknown and about which the works of the historians gave no precise information. Secondly it yielded vast quantities of material of all kinds—inscriptions, works of art, pottery, metal objects, coins. Some of this material, particularly the inscriptions, made a direct contribution to our knowledge of military, political or economic matters. The comparison and analysis of other material made it possible to establish a chronological classification of the pottery and other every-day objects, which was to prove a valuable guide to the historical interpretation of data recovered by excavation.

It has thus been possible not only to draw up detailed plans of Roman fortification works at a particular time but also to follow their development over the years. Even though at first the methods used did not have the meticulous accuracy of modern excavation techniques, which represent the application of the strict disciplines of prehistoric studies to what is necessarily a collective effort, they soon made notable strides. The excavators' picks brought to light not only stone-built walls but, more often than not, the less substantial remains of trenches, earthworks or post-holes; and the archaeologists thus learned to study the clues which might be provided by variations in the colour of the soil or differences between successive layers. Historical stratigraphy was not yet born, but researches of this kind led inevitably to its development.

Thus the mid 19th century marked a decisive stage in the transformation of the learned studies of the "antiquaries" into a practical and objective discipline making use of a wide range of techniques and specialisms in the pursuit of its objectives. This period saw the beginning of methodical excavation, and much of the work then begun was destined to continue for many years: some of it, indeed, into our own day. Mention may be made in particular of the excavations at Alise-Sainte-Reine, soon followed by those at Bibracte and Vertault, the initial impulse for which came, directly or indirectly, from Napoleon III.

The First Decades of the 20th Century

The early years of the 20th century, which saw the large-scale excavations of the *Limes* in Germany, were marked in France by the appearance of a number of large compendia of material and the first general surveys.

The Work of the Scholars

The production of the *Corpus* of Latin inscriptions (*CIL*, XII and XIII) by the Archaeological Institute of Berlin was facilitated and sometimes supplemented by numerous regional collections (e.g., those of L. Robert in the Moselle area, Camille Jullian at Bordeaux, Allmer and Dissard at Lyons). Then there was Espérandieu's *Collection of Bas-Reliefs, Statues and Busts of Roman Gaul*, published under the auspices of the Institut de France, a series of volumes which appeared over a period of some thirty years, with supplements which are still being issued in our own day. Joseph Déchelette, after producing his standard work on prehistory and protohistory, became one of the founders of the study of Gallo-Roman pottery, the methods of analysis and classification later being developed and refined by German and British scholars like Knorr and Oswald. The first works of synthesis also appeared at this time—Camille Jullian's monumental *History of Gaul* and Henri Hubert's work on the Celts. Camille Jullian has too often been dismissed as a historian of typical 19th century outlook: in fact his outstanding breadth of mind and masterly intuitions frequently opened up quite new avenues of research. Henri Hubert—familiar with the new disciplines of comparative linguistics and ethnology, a student of the Celtic languages, and himself a practising archaeologist—possessed a range of special skills rarely combined in a single scholar. He promoted research in a number of directions which were successfully followed by others after him, and remains an outstanding example and inspiration.

The work of Déchelette and Camille Jullian was continued by Albert Grenier, whose *Manual of Gallo-Roman Archaeology*, published from 1920 onwards, was a valuable compendium of the results of archaeological research and excavation in France. The final volumes of this monumental work were published after his death in 1962.

It must be admitted, however, that during this period—which in Germany and Switzerland saw much excavation work in progress, including such models of excavation technique as Gerhard Bersu's work on the Wittnauer Horn—there was little excavation of major significance in France. The State devoted only limited resources to the development of museums and field archaeology within France, and the organisation for carrying out archaeological research was almost non-existent. Almost all the available money went to excavations in North Africa and other areas outside France, which appealed to archaeologists with their promise of more spectacular results. In the early years of the 20th century archaeological activity in France was largely carried on in the study rather than the field.

The Pioneers of Field Archaeology

The current revival of interest in archaeological excavation in France, however, dates back considerably before the war. It was launched by a spontaneous movement, comprehending prehistory, protohistory and history within its scope, in which the first impulse came from individual enquirers with a wide range of different backgrounds, from a local doctor or chemist to ordinary countryfolk, many of them without scientific or academic training in archaeology. This indeed is the striking feature of the movement, that it seems to have been started by the enthusiasm of numbers of amateur archaeologists, fascinated by the remains of the past buried in the soil of France.

Among these pioneers a prominent place belongs to Saint-Just and Marthe Péquart, whose excavations in Brittany, particularly at Téviec and Hoedic, were models of careful technique, marking them out as initiators and forerunners of later developments. There were also peasants like Z. Le Rouzic, and later A. Brisson and A. Loppin, who, learning by experience, progressively built up a substantial body of knowledge, an unmatched experience of field work and an outstanding sharpness of observation. With the help and guidance of the Péquarts, Z. Le Rouzic did excellent work in the Carnac area, helping to establish the first reliable basis for the chronology of the protohistorical period in Brittany.

Brisson and Loppin, excavating in Champagne, an area which had long been a happy hunting ground for amateur diggers in search of collectors' pieces, were the first to realise that the structures hewn from the chalk were just as important as the objects they contained, and that it was essential to record and study them properly for the information they could yield about the civilisation, the technology, the economy and the religion of the people who had made them and used them. The energy and persistence of these two peasants, soon to be advised and guided by the lucid intelligence of Canon Favret, led to the recovery of hut bases, cemeteries, tombs, sanctuaries and the plans of *villae* and *vici*.

In southern France, following the brilliant discoveries by Dr Mouret at Ensérune and Brun at Glanum (Saint-Rémy), H. Rolland discovered and excavated the splendid Etrusco-Greek site of Saint-Blaise. Two vine-growers of Languedoc,

Odette and Jean Taffanel, devoted years of their lives to the archaeological exploration of their own village, Mailhac, discovering cemeteries and dwellings and throwing entirely fresh light on the protohistory of south-western France. A local schoolmaster, B. Sapène, was able by field work and research to reveal the topography and history of Lugdunum Convenarum (Saint-Bertrand-de-Comminges), and was fortunate enough to discover near his school the remains of an Augustan trophy *(Plates 95, 96)*—one of the most important French archaeological finds of the first half of the 20th century. Then, a few years before the war, Lagorgette identified the *oppidum* of Mont Lassois, near Vix (Côte d'Or); the work which he began here was continued by R. Joffroy and culminated in 1953 in the discovery of the magnificent tomb of the Princess of Vix *(Plates 15–18)*.

Thus the credit for the resumption of archaeological research and exploration in France in the years before the last war belongs entirely to amateur archaeologists such as these; and a rapid look through foreign archaeological literature is enough to show the value of the work they did. It was their efforts which gave a fresh impetus to Gallic and Gallo-Roman archaeology in the years between 1920 and 1940, at a time when the State was doing nothing to organise archaeological investigation or to provide it with the material resources it needed.

The New Organisation of Archaeological Research

The Statutory Basis

New statutory provisions relating to archaeological excavation and to casual finds of archaeological material were introduced by the Vichy government in 1942, and were subsequently confirmed after the Liberation. Finders of objects of archaeological interest were required to report them to the authorities, and no excavation was to be carried out without an official permit. The legislation established an embryonic archaeological service, dividing up the territory of France (at that time deprived of Alsace and Lorraine) into a number of regional departments of prehistoric and historical antiquities, each headed by a Director of Antiquities. The Director, a suitably qualified local person appointed by the Minister, was responsible for coordinating archaeological research in his district, supervising excava-

2

3

4

5

9

10

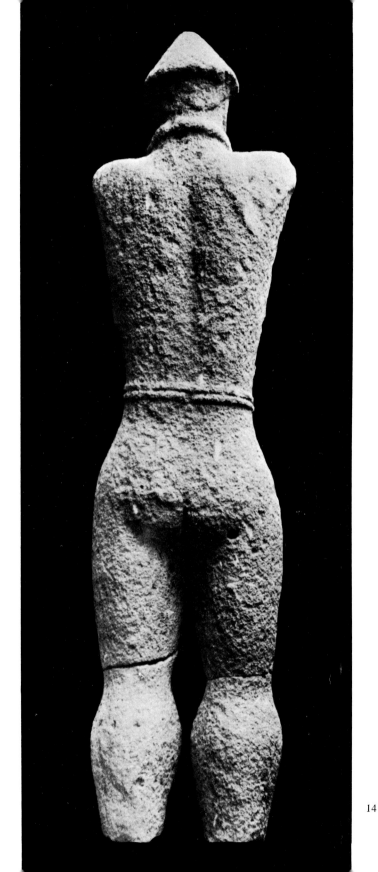

14

16

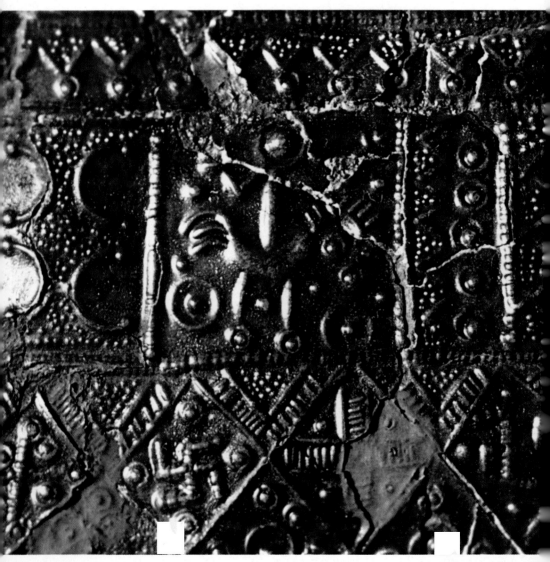

tions, carrying out archaeological work on behalf of the State, recording information about chance finds and publishing periodic reports on archaeological activities in his district in an official journal established by the Centre National de la Recherche Scientifique for the purpose. Administratively, he served as a link between practising archaeologists on the one hand and the central authorities on the other. A procedure for securing temporary entry to a site was provided so that the State could carry out excavations on important archaeological sites in spite of objections from the owners of the land, and the procedure for the compulsory purchase of land for public use was extended to include excavation sites. Notwithstanding its authoritarian character this legislation did not in fact establish an effective archaeological service, with its own establishment of specialised staff and the necessary accommodation and equipment; for the Directors of Antiquities were unpaid and had no staff or premises of their own.

The embryonic character of this organisation was in striking contrast to the pattern in neighbouring countries like Germany and Italy. In Italy the Soprintendenze alle Antichità established by the Fascist government were provided with trained staff, suitable accommodation and equipment, and extensive powers and resources. In Germany the provincial Departments of Antiquities *(Landesämter für Ur- und Frühgeschichte)*, also well provided with staff, equipment and financial resources, were reinforced by a network of excellently organised archaeological museums (at Trier, Bonn, Cologne and elsewhere), while the Römisch-Germanische Kommission in Frankfurt and the Römisch-Germanisches Zentralmuseum in Mainz served respectively as a source of inspiration and scientific guidance and as a central laboratory.

In spite of their limitations, however, the new French institutions did valuable work. They made it possible to extend the scale of archaeological research in France and to coordinate the work which had previously been carried on in isolation. They led to a more rapid exchange of information and promoted the training of excavators. And they had the particular merit that they drew the attention of the regional Directors of Antiquities, many of whom were university teachers and had been at the French Schools in Rome and Athens, both to the immense but neglected archaeological wealth of France and to the pitifully small resources which the government was prepared to devote to its excavation. The interests of Gallic and Gallo-Roman archaeology now found advocates much better equipped to defend them than the amateurs, the students of local history, the few enthusiastic pioneers who had hitherto stood almost alone in their efforts.

Current Developments

In recent years there has been a remarkable quickening in the pace of archaeological discovery, accompanied by important developments in methods and techniques which hold great promise for the future.

A number of factors can be recognised as contributing to these advances. First
among them is the progress of industrialisation. The large-scale earth-moving
operations made necessary by the laying out of new housing areas, the establishment of new industries and other developments (water supply, drainage and other
services, river improvements, and so on) are now carried out by mechanical
equipment, and in consequence the soil is being turned over on a much larger
scale than ever before. In agriculture the tractor-drawn subsoil ploughs now being
used cut more deeply into the ground than before. These developments have led
to an increase in the number of chance discoveries of archaeological material but
also, unfortunately, to an increase in the rate of destruction of archaeological sites.
In present circumstances, therefore, the main tasks of the archaeological service
are to keep in touch with major civil engineering operations, where necessary to
carry out emergency excavations on sites of known archaeological interest before
development takes place, to record all finds of archaeological material, to protect
important remains, and to ensure that the maximum amount of information is
obtained from such discoveries.

The second reason is connected with the growth of amateur archaeology, which
has undergone remarkable changes and has ever closer contacts with technical
experts and specialists. The general public is increasingly taking an interest in
archaeology and becoming increasingly well informed about it. This interest is
catered for by a considerable body of archaeological literature—much of it excellent—designed for the general reader. In this age of increased leisure archaeology
offers a spare-time occupation which combines physical exercise with intellectual
interest. Large numbers of people, therefore, have turned to archaeology as a
hobby, and many of them make a point of keeping up to date and using the most
modern and most accurate techniques, ranging from the use of light planes to
carry out air surveys to the most scientific excavation methods, not excluding
laboratory techniques.

Among these amateurs, for example, we find P. Parruzot of Sens developing the
techniques of air reconnaissance and photography best suited to the soil and

climatic conditions of the Yonne valley; R. Agache, in the Somme area, applying similar techniques to the conditions of the Picardy plateau *(Plates 6, 7)*; A. France-Lanord of Nancy developing methods of laboratory analysis suitable for application to weapons and other metal objects, and evolving an entirely new technique for the examination and dissection of specimens in the laboratory under binocular magnifying lenses, used in the excavations in the historic church of Saint-Denis, near Paris—the only means of preserving and studying such fragile and interesting remains as fragments of fabrics and embroidery; and A. Blanc of Valence combining his practical experience of archaeology with the special skills of the geologist and the chemist to develop techniques for the scientific analysis of pottery. Thus in a sense we are still in the age of the pioneer—with this difference that the amateur archaeologists of our day are often themselves in the forefront of technical progress, and that they not infrequently turn professional and are taken on to the strength of the Centre National de la Recherche Scientifique or the government archaeological service.

It must be added that there is now increasing scope for the employment of professional archaeologists, whether they are recruited from academic circles or from among field workers. The archaeological service, so ill equipped in its early days, is steadily expanding its resources and increasing its establishment of trained staff. The headquarters staff has recently been reorganised and an Excavation Division has been established under the immediate control of the Ministry of Cultural Affairs. Considerably increased financial resources have been made available, the regional Departments of Antiquities are being provided with the equipment they need, and staff is being trained for these departments so that the Directors of Antiquities may be relieved of some of their day-to-day responsibilities.

Meanwhile, in the field of archaeological literature, the standard of the journal *Gallia* has risen steadily under the skilled and energetic editorship of Professor P. M. Duval of the Collège de France. Its series of special supplements now includes a number of monographs of outstanding quality—by P. Wuilleumier on the theatres of Lyons *(Plate 75)*, by H. Rolland on Glanum and Saint-Blaise *(Plate 8)*, by A. Piganiol on the cadastral records of Orange, etc. The recent publication in the same series of a collective study of the triumphal arch of Orange *(Plates 132–134)* is a striking demonstration of the increasingly important part played by the government archaeological service in the scientific study and proper care of the monuments of Gaul.

Future Needs

Much, however, still remains to be done, and there are still considerable deficiencies to be made good. Many general problems await solution, and necessary action is continually postponed, although other countries, perhaps backward in some other respects, are able to take effective action in this field and to provide the financial resources required. The teaching of special subjects related to the protohistorical and Gallo-Roman periods is not adequately catered for in the French universities and tends to fall outside the normal degree course. The excavation training schools are not organised on a national basis and their running is left to local initiative. The laboratory facilities for scientific analysis and restoration are inadequate. The museums have insufficient accommodation and staff to house, care for, catalogue and study the vast quantities of material which are being discovered. The establishment of storage depots is no more than a stopgap, for their contents must sooner or later be passed on the museums, already overloaded as they are.

In short, although the archaeological service is now coming into effective operation, thanks to the efforts both of the authorities and of practising archaeologists, it has still to establish a solid base in the field of higher education and in the museums. The problems involved are exceedingly complex, and there are no solutions ready to hand; for in this respect France has more than half a century's leeway to make good.

This was clearly demonstrated in 1963, when some of the rooms at the Museum of National Antiquities at Saint-Germain-en-Laye were reopened to the public after reorganisation. The new arrangement of these rooms, carried out at considerable expense, was generally applauded for its novelty and ingenuity; but to some visitors, particularly scholars from other countries, it seemed to have suffered from the undue haste with which it had been carried out. It was felt also that in the arrangement of the rooms the ideas of the architects and decorators had apparently carried more weight than those of the archaeologists. It must be allowed, at any rate, that, in both its positive and its negative aspects, the experience has its lessons for the future.

Other less ambitious enterprises, like the Musée des Docks at Marseilles and the recently reorganised museums at Bourges, Epernay, Dijon, Metz and Strasbourg, are content with more modest standards of display but are better suited to the requirements of the public and of students and to the needs of research. The organisation of archaeological museums is not a matter for amateurs: a considerable period of practical training is required if the job is to be properly done. Long and painstaking effort is involved in cataloguing large numbers of objects of very different types, arranging them in a chronological series and carrying out a proper historical examination and analysis. The selection and arrangement of the exhibits is a matter in which the skills of the scientist, the teacher and the artist have to be combined; and it may not always be easy to reconcile their varying requirements.

In any account of the present situation in archaeology one important factor must not be forgotten—the need so generally and so deeply felt by scholars and students for regular contacts and exchanges of views with their colleagues. Conferences of the traditional type, like the annual meetings of the various learned societies, seem to have had their day: the preference nowadays is for smaller gatherings with a more restricted agenda. Meetings of this kind make it easier to achieve properly structured discussions, a useful exchange of information and opinion, and a thorough examination of the questions at issue.

Numerous meetings of this kind are now held, usually taking one or other of two forms. First there are regional conferences which bring together the archaeologists and excavators working in a particular area (e.g., Burgundy or Alsace-Lorraine), enabling them to get to know one another, to exchange information, to discuss their finds and to seek advice from colleagues. Papers are given by the various participants outlining their methods and summarising their results. Experience has shown that conferences of this type are an effective and helpful means of coordinating efforts and advancing knowledge. The other type of conference is designed to bring together archaeologists from different areas for the discussion of particular problems in certain specialised fields—the study of pottery, the problems of the protohistorical period, and so on. Examples of this type are the conferences devoted to the problems of the Rhône and Rhine areas, the meetings organised by the Society of National Antiquities, the conferences of the Dijon study group on ancient pottery in Gaul, and so on. These various meetings and conferences usually combine discussion sessions with visits to museums and excavation sites. In recent years they have made an important contribution to the training of archaeologists, the development of new techniques and the standardisation of methods.

METHODS AND TECHNIQUES

II

As we have noted, improvements in archaeological method, the development of new techniques and the spread of new ideas have depended much more on the enthusiasm of individuals than on the issue of guidance by the experts. It must be noted in passing, however, that knowledge of methods and techniques is still very unevenly distributed and that there are considerable disparities between different areas.

We shall consider in turn methods of prospecting, techniques of excavation, and the scientific analysis of the material recovered.

Methods of Prospecting

Surface Examination

Methodical prospecting is essentially based on the skills of the field archaeologist: that is, the art of interpreting the irregularities of the ground, differences in soil colouring and the pattern of vegetation cover to reveal the infilled ditch, the buried wall, the building or settlement concealed beneath a barely perceptible rise in the ground. This is the starting point of any methodical exploration, and in particular it is a necessary preliminary to properly conducted air reconnaissance; it is surface examination of this kind that leads to the discovery of sites previously unknown. Some archaeologists of peasant origin like A. Stieber in Alsace or A. Brisson in Champagne have acquired remarkable skill in observing differences of soil colour in ploughed land and are able to identify hut bases and sometimes even buried tombs with almost unerring accuracy. Examination on the ground must be supplemented by study of large-scale maps (in France the General Staff maps at a scale of 1:25,000) and local land registers for periods before recent redistributions of agricultural land. These older registers record place names and field systems which are often of interest as reflecting earlier patterns of land use.

Air Photography

Air photography for the purposes of archaeology may take two very different forms. One technique, which in the arid landscapes of Africa and Syria led to the spectacular revelation of the Roman *limes*, consists in the detailed examination in a stereoscopic viewer of photographs taken in special sorties by the Institut

Géographique National (a government agency), usually from high altitude. This method, as practised and developed by Col. Baradez, the author of an excellent study of the *Fossatum Africae*, requires long training and considerable experience, such as can be derived from photo-interpretation for military purposes. It must be conceded that in areas with a substantial depth of alluvial deposits, where the soil has been intensively cultivated over a long period, is largely concealed by vegetation or trees, or is continually exposed to the action of water, this method has not yielded such considerable results as in some of the semi-desertic regions bordering the Mediterranean. It is, however, an indispensable means of tracing and mapping the exact layout of such major features as the lines of roads or water channels, plans of towns or the remains of ancient field systems (e.g., Roman patterns of centuriation).

Whereas this technique is based on the examination of air photographs taken vertically from high altitude, the second method depends on the use of photographs, usually oblique, taken at low altitude. Although this method is less accurate, and cannot be used directly for the mapping of an area by photogrammetry, it is better suited to the soil and climatic conditions of Europe. In Britain and, more recently, in France and Germany, it has achieved substantial results. Two different methods of use have been developed, each appropriate to a different type of terrain. In valley areas with a covering of alluvial gravel air photography is used to study differences in the colouring of the vegetation when the crops are making their first growth (April–May), when they are fully ripe (July–August) or at the end of the season when there is a growth of secondary vegetation in the stubble fields (September–November). This method, developed by P. Parruzot in the Sens area and the Yonne valley, has yielded some spectacular results; in particular it has revealed an impressive number of cemeteries and settlements. On limestone plateaux with a covering of silt, however, it has proved more profitable to study differences in the colouring of the soil itself after ploughing. The process of ploughing, particularly the deep ploughing which is now commonly practised, shows up foundation materials as white markings on a dark ground, while ditches or trenches appear as darker lines, particularly at times when wet ground is drying out. The use of this method enabled R. Agache to identify a considerable number of Roman villas and protohistorical sites in the Somme area *(Plates 6, 7)*. But whichever of these two methods is used it is essential to prepare the ground properly in advance, to mark out carefully the areas to be photographed and to maintain close contact with the pilot of the aircraft so that the photographs are taken at exactly the right time.

It is a matter of some difficulty to determine the precise area to be excavated following air reconnaissance. At this stage it may be helpful to carry out soundings on the ground, using either an iron rod as a hand probe, as is the traditional practice in Champagne, or a helicoidal drill which brings up core samples from some depth.

Geophysical Methods

Other methods of prospecting have been developed by geophysicists in recent years. One such method involves measuring the resistivity of the soil by sticking copper pegs into the ground at regular intervals and passing an electric current between them. A series of measurements is plotted to give a resistivity curve, and from this can be deduced the existence of ditches or buried walls, which produce perceptible changes in the quantity of current passing between the electrodes.

Another method is based on the measurement of magnetism, either with the aid of mine detectors or with a proton magnetometer. By this means it is possible to locate deposits of iron or (since pottery has as a rule a fairly high level of magnetism) potters' kilns or waste heaps of ancient pottery.

In short, archaeologists now have at their disposal methods of prospecting and exploration which are efficient and accurate, but which require careful preparation and experienced operators. These methods are, therefore, still used on a relatively small scale. Yet at a time when so much destruction is being caused by mechanical earth-moving equipment it is vitally important that steps should be taken to locate archaeological sites by the most up-to-date and efficient methods available so that the areas most in need of protection can be identified.

Techniques of Excavation

Archaeologists have been slow to realise the irreversible nature of excavation and the fragility of the evidence it yields. An archaeological site is a book which cannot be read without destroying it in the process; and moreover it is a book which must be read backwards, beginning at the end. Thus the archaeologist approaches the exploration of a site with a sense of responsibility and almost of apprehension—in a state of mind perhaps not unlike that of a detective on the scene of a crime. He cannot afford to overlook any clue, and everything must be recorded before he destroys evidence whose significance he may not appreciate until much later.

The Lessons of Prehistoric Archaeology

It is fair to say that the high standard of completeness, accuracy, meticulous care and objectivity achieved by modern excavation methods is almost entirely due to the prehistorians. Starting off without any written sources, and for the most part without coherent structures, they were obliged to use every scrap of information that could be wrested from the earth, and could not afford to neglect the slightest piece of evidence, however insignificant it might appear at first sight. Thus it is mainly to the excavations of prehistoric sites that we owe the two fundamental conceptions which are the basis of any scientific excavation: the study of micro-topography, which enables us to recover the immediate setting of human activities (for example to picture for ourselves, some hundreds or thousands of years after the event, the craftsman plying his trade or the worshipper doing reverence to his gods), and the principle of stratigraphy, which makes it possible to establish the chronological succession of the generations. On the basis of these two concepts archaeologists have developed the technique of three-dimensional recording, with a horizontal grid for locating the position of objects on the surface and a spirit level or theodolite to determine levels. It is essential during the process of excavation to fix with the maximum degree of precision the position of every object of any importance, of every fragment of a structure, of every scrap of evidence, so that we can attempt to establish the condition of the site and the positions of the various objects before the destructions and the changes brought about during the passage of time. It may then be possible to draw conclusions which will give us a fuller and deeper understanding of man in his social setting and in the process of development. For all the archaeologist's anxious thought and painstaking labour is directed towards a single aim—to understand the nature of man as it finds physical expression in the results of his activities and his speculations and in the products of his industry, without passing through the distorting medium of written texts or other documents, tendentious or misleading as they so often are.

The technique of stratigraphic excavation grew directly out of the exploration of prehistoric sites; for in a cave shelter the archaeological layers are superimposed on one another, separated by sterile levels (rock falls, alluvium deposited by floods, etc.). The importance of stratigraphy was confirmed when archaeologists tackled the stratified sites of the Near East: the *tells* of Mesopotamia and Syria, built up by the successive construction, destruction and reconstruction of a series of settlements, provided ideal opportunities for applying the method to protohistorical and historical civilisations, and the tablets, inscriptions on stone, works of art and other dated objects found in them soon introduced an absolute chronology into the succession. It was not at once realised that the town sites of Gaul and some of the *oppida* of the Celtic period also showed a stratigraphic sequence, frequently of considerable depth with as many as twenty identifiable levels. This can be illustrated from the example of Strasbourg, where the first isolated stratigraphic observations were made before 1870 but real progress in identifying the ancient levels became possible only in 1899, as a result of cooperation between the city engineer's department and local archaeologists. Strasbourg *(Plates 1–5)* was a particularly promising site, since the town was established by the Celts and developed by the Romans on a number of low-lying islets in the arms of a river, so that its construction involved a good deal of building up of the ground level. The site can be compared to a *millefeuille* pastry composed of a succession of layers of puff paste, cream and sugar. Over most of the area we have been able to distinguish fourteen successive layers, and in the most favourable conditions (where the later Roman levels are still overlaid by early mediaeval levels) the number rises to twenty or more.

"Graduated" Excavation (Fouille en Gradins)

Theoretically the technique of stratigraphic excavation consists in stripping off successive layers horizontally one after the other over an extensive area, taking care to record all remains of buildings, structures and other objects encountered at each level and collecting all material which may be useful for dating purposes —coins, sherds of pottery, bronze objects, and so on. In practice, however, for a variety of reasons, it is not as simple as this. In the first place, the sites available in built-up areas are not large enough to allow of large-scale horizontal stripping, which is possible only in open country. Moreover within the excavation area there are always a variety of obstacles interrupting the continuity of the archaeological layers, particularly deep basement or cellar structures which may date from various different periods. Finally, since the deposits may not be in uniform horizontal layers but may be quite irregular, and since it is not always easy to distinguish one level from another, it is desirable not to stick to straightforward horizontal stripping but to combine this with trenching in depth. Only in this way is it possible to distinguish quickly the local pattern of stratigraphy and to observe its irregularities. The method can be described as graduated excavation *(fouille en gradins)*. It has obvious analogies with the techniques of dissection employed in the study of plants or animals. Its great merits are its flexibility and its ready adaptability to the facts of the situation, however variable and unexpected these may be.

Graduated excavation involves a number of successive operations—the removal of recent deposits and layers of mixed composition, the systematic stripping of successive surface layers, the digging of trial trenches for stratigraphic purposes, the actual process of graduated excavation in successive "tiers", and the detailed study and recording of stratigraphic sections. The trial trenches are so drawn as to cover the whole of the site under investigation, giving a rough idea of its average depth and its general structure. Starting from these trenches, the excavators then strip selected areas layer by layer, leaving stratigraphic indicators *(témoins)* at places where there are remains of structures. This produces a series of steps or tiers which give a general picture of the different levels, showing their surface appearance and their relationship in depth; and it is perhaps in this respect that the technique most resembles that of dissection. Photographs are taken throughout these various operations so as to give a clear and accurate idea of the sequence of periods and of the various remains. Finally the last *témoins* are removed and the various exposed sections are recorded. The "reading" of the stratigraphic sections, aided as it is by the evidence produced by the excavations, is a difficult art which can be acquired only by long experience. Levels must be determined by reference to a single bench-mark adopted as standard for all urban sites. In Strasbourg this is the level used by the towns in the Rhine valley; elsewhere it is likely to be the standard spot level used in France.

Historical Interpretation

The various layers can be dated by systematic examination of the pottery, everyday objects and coins discovered in successive levels. All this material is stored in boxes, classified according to the different layers and to the squares of the grid into which the site is divided, and is then drawn and catalogued. Constant watchfulness and rigorous method are necessary to maintain the stratigraphic classification of the material, which passes through many hands during the processes of washing, drying, marking and putting into store. All this requires a good deal of time and manpower. In any reasonably productive excavation some five or ten times as long is required for the classification and study of the material as for the excavation itself. The modern method of stratigraphic excavation thus makes considerably increased demands on the excavator; and it cannot be said that these demands are invariably met in the excavations now being undertaken.

The results of the excavation will be recorded on a series of record sheets and drawings of stratigraphic sections, noting the spot height, general character (habitation level, infill material, accumulation of debris, destruction or conflagration level, floor surface, etc.) and date of the various layers. Comparisons between sections taken from different parts of the site make it possible to build up a more general impression of a considerable area on the basis of a limited number of exploratory digs. A comparative study of the levels often produces unexpected insights into the topography, history or way of life of a settlement at different stages of its existence; and comparison of the stratigraphy of different sites may suggest even more far-reaching conclusions on the history of the region, the succession of invasions and destructions, the phases of purposeful rebuilding, and even climatic or tectonic changes (e.g., periods of drought or landslides) during historic times.

Thus at Strasbourg, by studying the levels of the sanctuary square, the *via praetoria* and a drainage trench running parallel to it, and the buildings along the *via* inside the camp, we were able to establish the history of the changes in drainage systems over the whole Roman period, and could observe the efforts of the Roman engineers to avoid the accumulation of mud and the consequent obstruction of the square and the road. Similarly by comparing stratigraphic sections from Strasbourg, Ehl and Biesheim-Künheim we found evidence for a long series of spates of the Rhine between 60 and 160 A.D. Elsewhere the matching of conflagration and destruction levels at different sites has made it possible to fix the dates of various invasions and military mutinies, which were for the most part already known but sometimes raised difficult problems.

Thus historical stratigraphy is a living and concrete study which enables us to draw valid historical conclusions. When the excavator encounters accumulations of broken tiles showing signs of burning, or the remains of burned mud walls in a layer of ashes and charred wood, or finds weapons and ballista missiles, coins and intact pottery vessels abandoned by soldiers in the tumult and confusion of battle, he is able to visualise the clash of conflict and the destruction wrought by mutinous troops or savage barbarians. Noting in a stratigraphic section the thick layers of gravel and building stones carried away by a river in spate, he can picture the agitation of the inhabitants as they watched the menacing rise of the water. Historical stratigraphy offers a vivid means of recovering history from the earth, and often makes it possible to add to the historical record chapters which were previously unknown or ignored or deliberately suppressed.

The Excavation of Tombs

As we have seen, the study of large town sites calls for proper excavation tech-niques, constant vigilance and a high degree of organisation; but even greater care and an even more meticulous approach are required in the investigation of ceme-teries, tombs and cult sites, where the traces left by burial practices or acts of worship may throw light on the religious beliefs of the peoples concerned.

Great strides have been made by Dutch, German and British excavators during the last thirty years in the technique for the exploration of burial mounds. Such high technical standards are now required for the excavation of burials, however, that it is frequently not possible to do the work satisfactorily in field conditions, at the mercy of the weather and the depredations of clandestine diggers. This may then lead the archaeologist, as in the investigation of the Merovingian tombs at Saint-Denis by A. France-Lanord, to transfer the excavation to the laboratory, where the work can be carried on at leisure, unhampered by extraneous difficulties. There are various ways of doing this. Sometimes the entire burial is cut out of the ground, along with the immediately surrounding soil; the whole thing is then strengthened and bound together with a plastic substance and thereafter removed to the laboratory, where it can be carefully examined and photographed under X-rays before being meticulously dissected with a scalpel under binocular magni-fying lenses. Alternatively, where it is not possible to deal with the whole of the tomb and its contents in this way, it is divided into sections, which are then sup-ported on sheets of metal and transferred to the laboratory. Finally there is a still more radical method, recently adopted in Germany for the excavation of a cult site of great interest, the votive pit of Holzhausen. This involves erecting over the excavation site a temporary laboratory, of light construction but with well insulated walls and equipped with electric power, heating and lighting. The scientific exami-nation of the site can then be carried on under shelter, in conditions which facilitate the use of the most intricate and delicate procedures.

An important excavation like that of the tomb of Vix was carried out by R. Joffroy with great competence in the most unfavourable conditions; and it is quite certain that the work would be done very differently now. A laboratory of plastic material on a metal frame, with double walls for heat insulation and with heating, lighting and all the technical equipment necessary for scientific examination and photo-graphy, would be built round the tomb at once. The excavation would take a year, or perhaps more. The whole of the magma (the produce of decomposition) on the floor of the tomb would be carefully examined *in situ* with binocular magnifying lenses and then photographed. Everything in the tomb—organic remains, fragments of fabrics, traces left by perishable materials—would be subjected to laboratory examination in this way. Chemical analysis would make it possible to detect traces of colouring matter or even of perfumes. Thanks to modern technological developments, resources of this kind can readily be enlisted in the investigation of sites of major interest and significance.

Underwater Excavation

Finally mention must be made of a relatively new field which is now in course of rapid development—underwater excavation. Since the invention of the Cousteau-Gagnan aqualung underwater excavation off the Mediterranean coasts has developed on a considerable scale. Good work has been done not only under official auspices but also by amateur divers, some of whom have shown a genuine spirit of scientific enquiry. The first properly organised experiments in the examination of wrecks were carried out at the Grand Congloué, near Marseilles, in 1952 and off the Ile du Levant in 1957. A technique was evolved for the clearance of silt with the help of a suction tube operated by a compressor. As F. Benoit has observed, the excavation of an underwater site—offering a rich store of material of all kinds in a reasonably good state of preservation, all securely assignable to the same period—is not merely aimed at bringing in a large haul of amphoras. It involves a methodical survey of the site and the preparation of a complete record, accompanied by photographs, of the framework of the ship, so far as this has survived, and of the cargo. The aim must be to achieve the fullest and most accurate picture possible of the ship, including its hull structure, if possible its rigging, the stowage of the cargo, and all the information that can be gleaned for the precise dating of the wreck.

In other words, underwater excavation must maintain the same standards as excavation on land, with the added difficulty that the excavator's mental activity and reactions are hampered by the watery element in which he finds himself, and that he cannot work for longer than 25 minutes at depths greater than 40 metres. Nevertheless special techniques for recording the positions of objects under water have been developed in order to simplify his task. One method, used by Italian excavators working on a wreck off the island of Spargi, is to lower on to the sea bed a large net with meshes of uniform size (1 to 2 metres square) and to peg it out over the "tumulus" formed by the wreck so as to provide a grid on which the whole excavation, including all structures and objects found, can be plotted. Another method which has its supporters is to depend entirely on photography, taking a series of stereoscopic views so that it is possible to build up a complete record by the use of photogrammetry. But even if satisfactory methods of applying this technique can be devised it can never be a substitute for a proper topographical survey and three-dimensional recording, though it may provide a useful cross-check on the observations of the excavators.

There is no doubt, however, that the use of "houses under the sea", as recently conceived and tried out by Commander Cousteau, will make it possible in future to carry out underwater excavation more rapidly and to attain a degree of precision and objectivity comparable with that achieved in excavations on land, since it will almost entirely overcome what has been the greatest handicap to underwater excavation—the short length of time for which divers can operate at a stretch.

Auxiliary Techniques

The development of stratigraphic excavation and underwater exploration has led to rapid and spectacular progress in a specialised field which was until recently neglected but is now taking an important place among the auxiliary disciplines of the historian—ceramography, the scientific study of pottery. In H. P. Eydoux's apt and striking phrase, "pottery is to the archaeologist what a white stick is to a blind man". The sherd or, if he is lucky, the intact vessel which he finds—or, more accurately, the series of such finds—enables him to date the archaeological layer in which they occur, and thus also to date the event which the layer records.

Modern Ceramographic Methods

Accordingly archaeologists have devoted a good deal of attention to pottery, the "type fossil" which is so commonly yielded by their excavations. (Sometimes, indeed, it is almost embarrassingly abundant, so that the store-rooms of our museums can barely cope with the flood of material). They have given close study to the shapes and profiles, seeking to determine the influence of custom and fashion in the varying styles, attempting to trace a line of development which reflects the vicissitudes of economic life and the great events of history. They have then tried to identify the output of particular workshops and even the individual potter responsible for producing a particular vase.

One type of pottery which has been particularly studied is what used to be known as Samian or false Samian ware and is now called *terra sigillata (Plates 193, 194)*. This ware, covered with a tough and impermeable slip of brilliant red, was produced in very large quantities in the workshops of Gaul. It often bears potters' marks, and may also be decorated with patterns stamped in relief. The decoration itself and the stamps used to produce it can be studied and systematically compared, making it possible, thanks to the excavations of pottery-making establishments, to identify the place of manufacture and the particular workshop. The study of *sigillata* ware, indeed, is becoming a specialty in its own right, founded on the analysis of the characteristics of the stamps used and of their association, which makes it possible to identify the repertoire and style of individual workshops and even individual potters.

More recently the composition of the paste and the tempering material has been studied by means of physical and chemical analysis. The proportion of silica, the coefficient of expansion at different temperatures and the presence of certain rare minerals or fossils enables us to establish the place of origin of the pottery. Moreover firing experiments and physico-chemical studies have enabled the techniques of manufacture, particularly of *sigillata* ware, to be deduced with a high degree of probability. It has been noted that techniques seem to have varied in the course of time, and in particular that there was a considerable increase in firing temperature at a certain period. Finally, chemical micro-analysis has made it possible to detect in certain types of pottery vessels, particularly amphoras, traces of the foodstuffs they contained (oil, wine, *garum*, etc.).

These are all recent and very promising fields of research; and other new techniques of analysis, simple and relatively inexpensive, are in process of being developed, particularly by A. Blanc of Valence, Picon of Lyons and Cabotse of Moulins. A whole new world is being opened up to systematic research, a world rich in promise for the study of technological and economic development.

Residual Radioactivity and Remanent Magnetism

Although they do not yet directly concern the Gallic and Gallo-Roman periods, it would not be right to omit mention of such ultra-modern techniques for the analysis of matter as the study of residual radioactivity and remanent magnetism. The determination of residual radioactivity, which consists in measuring the activity of a substance which remains radioactive for a long period, carbon 14, produces datings which have completely renewed the chronology and the historical pattern of the Neolithic period and the Early and Middle Bronze Ages. The technique is, however, a difficult one to apply, and the results it produces are often uncertain, showing a lack of precision for the period between the 8th century B.C. and the 4th century A.D. For this period, however, the synchronisms which have been established with the chronologies of the Mediterranean civilisations, based on the occurrence of metal objects and pottery from the Middle East, Etruria and Greece in tombs and occupation levels in western Europe, provide a sufficiently accurate system of dating.

Research is in progress under the direction of M. Thellier, Director of the Institut de Physique du Globe in Paris, with the object of establishing the pattern of changes in the terrestrial magnetic field in protohistorical and historical times by measuring and studying the orientation of the magnetic field in ceramic material. This approach is based on the fact that as it cools after firing baked clay takes on the magnetism of its period, so that potters' kilns and to some extent also the pottery produced in them preserve a fossil magnetic field. It is evidently important for the geophysicists to determine past variations in terrestrial magnetism; but it would be no less valuable for the archaeologist to know the direction of the field and its intensity at different periods, for this could provide the basis of a technique of dating which would usefully supplement and refine the datings obtained from radiocarbon determinations. This stage has not yet, however, been reached.

The Contribution of the Natural Sciences

The natural sciences are also making their contribution to the progress of archaeology by providing additional information to assist the excavator. Palynology, the analysis of fossil pollen found in archaeological levels, can sometimes afford evidence of climatic changes in protohistorical and historical times. The period of heavy rainfall which seems to have had such profound repercussions on human activity about the year 800 B.C. was first detected by the palaeobotanists, and it is to them that we must look for information on the clearance of land for cultivation at certain periods for which we have little in the way of written sources. The identification and statistical analysis of animal bones found on dated occupation sites, too, can give us some idea of the main activities of the inhabitants (hunting, fishing, stock-rearing, etc.), and if methodically pursued can even be made to yield evidence on the history of the various domestic species and the exchanges between different regions. Even the tiny mollusc shells found in the different levels, if identified and analysed, can lead to interesting deductions about the local climate and even about the topography of the area in ancient times (the proximity of water, the existence of shade, and so on).

There is thus wide scope for cooperation between archaeology and other scientific disciplines, opening up an immense field of research, and it is unfortunate that the development of this collaboration is held back by inadequacy of laboratory facilities and shortage of trained staff.

SOME PROBLEMS IN THE HISTORY OF CIVILISATION

III

It is unnecessary to attempt a detailed survey of a field of study which is now well established, particularly when we have such excellent textbooks as those of Déchelette and Grenier which—though in some respects out of date—bring together the essential facts and bibliographical information for readers who desire to study particular questions more thoroughly. In this chapter we shall merely pick out one or two of the most important problems and seek to outline the contribution which current research and discovery are making to their solution. This may involve giving a good deal of attention to some current work and ignoring other work of equal significance: it should be made clear, therefore, that omissions of this kind do not imply any value judgment.

The Main Themes of Research

The general problems presented by Gallic and Gallo-Roman archaeology are evidently numerous and diverse, but they can be related to a number of dominant themes. The first of these is *continuity*. When Gaul was conquered by Rome it had a centuries-old culture and firmly established traditions in which certain technical skills were associated with particular stylistic trends in art and with particular religious beliefs and practices: we are led, therefore, to enquire whether the special features of this native culture disappeared after the conquest.

Secondly, there is the question of *assimilation*. We are surprised to observe how quickly the people of Gaul adopted the language of their conquerors, became integrated into the political life of the Empire, fought in its defence, assimilated Roman technical skills and adapted themselves to the Roman way of life. Was this assimilation complete and universal? Can we identify the social mechanisms of romanisation on the one hand, and can we also detect a certain resistance to the process of romanisation? Were certain periods more favourable to romanisation, while others saw a reaction towards the native culture, or even a resurgence of Gallic traditions?

Finally there is the question of *origins*; for the two fundamental questions which we have just defined cannot be answered without the fullest knowledge of the pattern of indigenous life before the conquest and the complex of traditions which the native culture brought with it into the melting pot of romanisation. We shall thus find it necessary to consider the origins of Gallic culture in the protohistorical period, from the earliest stage at which it is possible to establish its chronology with sufficient accuracy. How did the Gauls acquire the skills which made them one of the most advanced peoples in the western world? What were the origins of their agriculture, their industries, their communal activities, their trade, their art, their religion? In the present state of knowledge archaeology is very far from being able to give complete, objective and precise answers to these difficult problems. It is, however, possible to give a general picture of the present state and future prospects of archaeological research, without glossing over the fact that in many fields our ignorance is greater than our knowledge.

Continuity, assimilation, the origins of the native culture: such are the main themes of this chapter. In discussing them we shall seek to indicate what light has been thrown on them by recent discoveries and current research, steering as impartial and objective a course as possible between opposing theories. Some scholars maintain that the Gauls retained their national identity intact behind the artificial façade of romanisation; others believe that Gaul was thoroughly assimilated and that little of the genuine native culture survived. It is our aim to understand by what process of development and what social mechanisms the native culture, the elements contributed by Rome and the influences emanating from neighbouring provinces came together to create the new reality, varied in pattern and constantly changing throughout its history, which constituted the provincial civilisation of Gaul.

The Question of Origins

In considering the problem of the origin of the Celts and their settlement in Gaul present-day archaeology tends to reject the historical theories, sometimes based on linguistic evidence, of such scholars as Arbois de Jubainville and Camille Jullian and to rely instead on the interpretation of the distribution maps for different kinds of material—metal objects (bronze ornaments, weapons and implements), burial practices, pottery, and so on.

The Proto-Celts

Since the last war the study of the protohistory of Gaul has made considerable strides in France as a result of the contact and cooperation which has been established between French and German scholars. It was the publication in the *Revue Archéologique de l'Est* of an important study by W. Kimmig on the Urnfield culture in France which in a sense launched the movement, making it possible ot fit earlier finds in eastern and central Gaul into the chronological framework established for southern Germany and central Europe. Moreover this framework has itself been considerably refined during the last twenty years by the important work which has been done on the basis of comparisons with dated finds from the countries round the Mediterranean (Müller-Karpe, Kossack). Thus by a process of gradual extension Gallic chronology is being linked up with the chronologies of Egypt and the Middle East. It is becoming steadily clearer that there is a synchronism between the Indo-European invasions of western Europe and the Balkans on the one hand and of the Aegean world and Asia Minor on the other. And so on the basis of chronological typology and comparative archaeology wide new historical perspectives are being opened up.

The movement of the Proto-Celts into western Europe about 1500 B.C. has been linked with the Achaean invasion and the emergence of Mycenaean civilisation. It is certain, at any rate, that there is a synchronism between the Proto-Celtic tumulus culture of southern Germany and Mycenaean civilisation. Amber spacerbeads of Kakovatos type have been found in tumuli in southern Germany and Alsace. Some of these are to be seen in the Haguenau museum; they may be dated to the 14th century B.C. Similarly the invasions of the Urnfield peoples (1250 to 1000 B.C.) which radically transformed western Europe and the Proto-Celtic world at the end of the Bronze Age have been linked with the invasions of the Dorians in mainland Greece and the Sea Peoples in the Middle East.

In the light of recent discovery and research it appears that the Celtic settlement in Gaul took place in a series of waves from southern Germany and Alsace from the middle of the Bronze Age (1500 B.C.) onwards. From this early period the Proto-Celtic tumulus culture spread towards the south-west (Charente) by way of the southern Paris basin and Normandy. The finds made by Abbé Philippe at Fort Harrouard, and more recently those of G. Bailloud in the forest of Fontainebleau, show that the Proto-Celtic culture of the Middle Bronze Age, represented by its pottery and certain types of bronze pin, was already established to the south of Paris between 1500 and 1200 B.C. This may perhaps have been a first wave of invaders; but in the present state of knowledge only sporadic traces of their presence are known.

The Advance of the Urnfield Culture

It is mainly for the Urnfield period that recent research has contributed important new information and opened up fresh vistas. The changes in burial rites which took place from the end of the Bronze Age onwards, with inhumation in tumulus tombs giving place to cremation in flat graves, combined with the appearance of new pottery types quite different from those of the earlier period and the progress made in bronze-working and particularly in casting techniques (involving the use of a clay core) and the beating of sheet metal, now seem to be closely connected with an invasion coming from Central Europe in a number of waves which progressively submerged southern Germany and eastern, central and southern Gaul. Earlier scholars like Déchelette and Hubert, although aware of the existence of this period (Déchelette's Bronze IV), had not realised its complexity, extent and importance—for its consequences continued to be felt into the Iron Age.

The first harbingers of the Urnfield invasion appear as early as 1300–1200 B.C. The distribution of certain typical objects—collared pins, bronze knives with riveted hilts, engraved bracelets with rounded ends—seem to point to considerable trading contacts, reaching far into southern Gaul, if not to a first wave of invaders. Between 1250 and 1200 B.C. the first tombs of the period which Kimmig calls the "preliminary Urnfield phase" appear in Burgundy and Champagne. They are particularly dense in the *départements* of Yonne, Aube and Côte-d'Or, an area always predestined to serve as a link between eastern and southern Gaul by way of the Saône and Rhône valleys.

The best known cemetery of this period is the one at La Colombine, the most interesting tombs in which were excavated by C. Bolnat between 1929 and 1939. These excavations were published by Abbé Lacroix, who interpreted the variety of burial rites (with inhumation still commoner than cremation) and the relatively crude pottery as indicating a mingling between an indigenous population of Neolithic tradition and Celtic incomers. It is unfortunate that our information about the tombs of this period in Gaul is so scanty, for conclusions of this kind would carry more conviction if they were supported by evidence obtained from the careful excavation of a number of different cemeteries, so as to provide adequate comparative material. The cemetery at La Colombine did, however, yield large quantities of metal objects, including a very fine diadem made from a boar's tusk mounted with bronze wire which is still unique of its kind, engraved bracelets with rounded and enlarged ends, a number of pins and a greave with spiral ornament, which have their counterparts in Alsace, Switzerland and southern Germany. The pottery, although relatively coarse, is closely related to that of the earliest Urnfield sites in the Rhône valley.

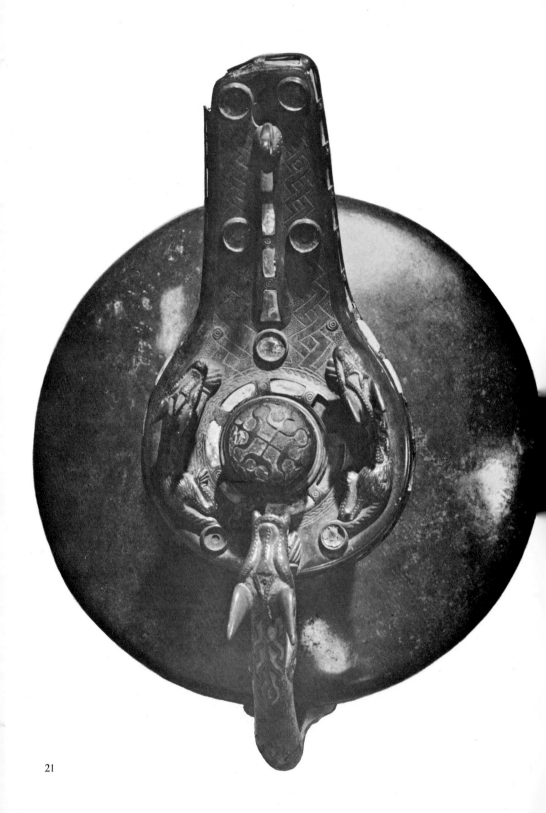

22

24

25

26

27

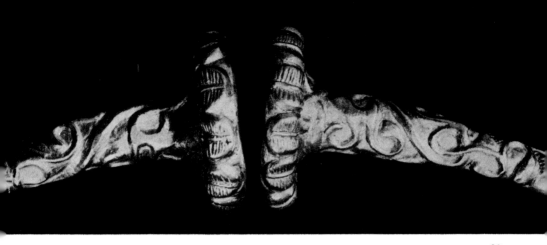

30

31

32

33

34

35

36

37

39

40

In more recent excavations by A. Brisson and A. Loppin in Champagne, near Epernay, the same pottery of the early Urnfield period has been found in hut bases. It is sometimes associated with pottery of Neolithic or Chalcolithic tradition, suggesting that the arrival of the Proto-Celts and their settlement in Champagne was not earlier than 1200 B.C.

Considered along with the cemeteries excavated at Aulnay-aux-Planches, these excavations demonstrate the importance of the area to the north and west of the Marais de Saint-Gond, on the borders of Champagne, the point of entry for invaders coming either from the upper Rhine or from the middle Rhine valley by way of the Moselle.

The Cemeteries of Aulnay-aux-Planches

The detailed study of the tombs and other structures found in the cemeteries of Aulnay-aux-Planches (Marne) has yielded a rich harvest of information not only on the chronology of the Gallic invasions and the process of settlement but on the burial rites and religion of the invaders. With the help of a chronology based on pottery types we can follow the progress of settlement by the incomers. The first evidence is provided by the establishment of a regular cemetery, with burials grouped in an orderly way, dating from about 950–900 B.C. Then, between 800 and 750 B.C., new settlers arrived from the Moselle and middle Rhine valleys. The new arrivals brought with them the practice of burial in tumuli surrounded by circular ditches, a practice inherited from the Proto-Celtic Bronze Age. The significant feature is the co-existence, side by side, of two different communities, one cremating their dead and burying them in flat graves, the other still using tumuli with circular ditches.

This site also yields evidence on the origins of the funerary cult and the ritual of sacrifice characteristic of the Gauls. In immediate proximity to a group cemetery with numbers of separate tombs was a large cult precinct, a kind of *temenos* surrounded by a ditch, containing two tombs set apart from the rest, no doubt belonging to priests or heroised chiefs, together with two inhumation graves each containing a skeleton with no grave goods (human sacrifices?) and a curious ritual feature with a sacrificial pit containing the skull and horns of an aurochs and a large shinbone from a bovid. In between these structures there had been lines of stelae on a fixed orientation, of which only a few traces were discovered. At this early period, therefore, about 950 B.C., we have evidence of a funerary cult in which divinities of the world beyond the grave were probably associated with dead leaders who were worshipped as heroes. This is an important discovery, for, as K. Schwartz has recently shown ("Zum Stand der Ausgrabungen in der spät-keltischen Viereckschanze von Holzhausen", in *Jahresbericht der bayerischen Denkmalpflege*, 1962, p. 55), it throws light on later developments: on this site we can recognise the origins of the Gallic funerary ritual which at a later stage, in the Iron Age and even during the Roman period, is attested by funerary chapels, temples in honour of heroes and divinities of the underworld, and the votive pits which are sometimes wrongly referred to as burial pits. These pits were in fact originally sacrificial pits whose function was to provide a means of communication between men and the subterranean powers which protected the dead and dispensed riches to men.

The excavations at Aulnay-aux-Planches are among the most important excavations carried out in the field of French protohistory, demonstrating how thorough field excavation can throw fresh light on a little known chapter in the story of Gallic origins.

The Awakening of the West

If a label had to be attached to the period between the 8th and 5th centuries B.C. perhaps the most appropriate one would be the "awakening of the West". This is a period of crucial importance in the development of the culture of Gaul; for it is during these centuries that the Celts make their appearance in history and create their own distinctive art and civilisation. During this period there was built up a body of tradition which developed throughout the Iron Age and persisted into Roman times.

The formation of this culture raises a great many problems which are by no means easy to resolve in the present state of knowledge, but the broad lines of development can be briefly stated. After the decline of the Urnfield culture at the end of the 8th century B.C. the continental Celtic world was dominated successively by two types of civilisation very different from one another: first the Hallstatt culture of the First Iron Age, then the La Tène culture of the Second Iron Age. The Hallstatt culture was extremely heterogeneous, and is found in numerous regional variants with many features of foreign origin. The La Tène culture, on the other hand, was from the outset an independent, homogeneous and national culture, with a powerful capacity for expansion, which extended its influence over much of Europe as a result of the migrations of the Gallic peoples. In the light of our present knowledge of the history of the continental Celtic peoples, how are such radical differences to be explained?

The Decline of the Urnfield Culture and the Thraco-Cimmerian Invasion

By the end of the 8th century B.C. the Urnfield culture in France was in a state of decline. It was a peasant culture, closely bound to the soil and with few contacts with the outside world. The society revealed by the tombs and hut bases found in Alsace and Champagne, for example, is depressingly mean and impoverished: there are few tombs which stand out from the rest by the richness of their furnishings, few metal objects in the burials or the dwellings. This impression is confirmed by the relative abundance of "founders' hoards" in the transitional period between the Late Bronze Age and the Early Hallstatt period. These frequently contain a high proportion of discarded objects cut into small pieces, suggesting that the bronze-working industry now depended mainly on the recovery of scrap metal.

The principal reason for this fall in the standard of living and the scarcity of metal may have been the catastrophic increase in rainfall about the year 800 B.C. which led to serious floods, submerging valleys and the shores of lakes and creating large areas of marsh and bog, and may have paralysed trade and interfered with agriculture. It is important to note, however, that this poverty-stricken culture of the late Urnfield period nevertheless survived for a very long period in certain areas in western, central, south-western and south-eastern Gaul which remained unaffected by the cultural influences flowing through the Celtic world between the 8th and 4th centuries B.C. In certain places it seems to have lingered on until the La Tène III phase (2nd century B.C.).

At the end of the 8th century B.C. the Thraco-Cimmerian invaders—horsemen from southern Russia, driven out of their homeland by the arrival of the Scythians —came into contact with the Celtic world. Some of them had passed through the Caucasus and made their way into Anatolia, where their arrival is recorded in the written sources. Another wave of incomers seems to have moved up the Danube valley into Hungary, from which some of them may have passed into Bavaria.

Their arrival in Hungary in considerable numbers is well attested. They brought with them a particular type of horse-bit, of Oriental origin. The same type of bit is found, however, in many tombs of the Early Hallstatt period in Bavaria and in a number of tombs in Belgium (Court-Saint-Etienne): must we therefore conclude that Thraco-Cimmerian horsemen settled in Bavaria and in northern Gaul, which was then occupied by various branches of the Celtic people? It seems doubtful whether these tombs are evidence of a movement of population into the areas concerned; it is more plausible to suppose that we are concerned here with the spread of technological innovations, including the introduction of new methods of using and training horses.

At any rate the arrival of these horsemen seems to have led to the development of a new social differentiation in the Celtic world, and to the emergence of an aristocratic caste of "knights" armed with iron swords; for at this period the richer type of tomb reappears, with furnishings which usually include harness and weapons. The farther to the west and south they are, the later the tombs appear to be. In Hungary some of them still belong to the last phase of the Urnfield culture. In Bavaria they date exclusively from the first phase of Early Hallstatt. In a tumulus near Chabestan (Hautes-Alpes) Courtois has recently found pieces of harness which appear to date from the end of the Early Hallstatt phase; and in Languedoc, at Mailhac, we have horsemen's tombs, with bits of rather different type, which can be dated to about 600 B.C. Odette Taffanel has suggested, very plausibly, that the horses were imported at the same time as these bits, which are associated with a complicated type of harness, possibly made to measure. Bits very similar to those found at Mailhac have also been recorded at Sesto Calende in northern Italy. In this case they were found in association with light two-wheeled fighting chariots of Etrusco-Illyrian type, probably dating from the middle of the 6th century B.C. This distribution in space and time is much easier to explain if we interpret it as the spread of a new fashion, a new technique for the training and control of horses. It can readily be understood that these innovations had social consequences. Between the 8th and the 6th century Gallic society seems to have undergone a process of differentiation, as a result of the rise to predominance of a caste of horsemen and later of chariot-riders. The occurrence in tombs of horse trappings and, later, of the remains of chariots is the distinctive mark of this new nobility. The rich tombs of Bavaria, Belgium, Languedoc, Switzerland and Burgundy, including the famous tomb of Vix, have usually one factor in common—the furnishings include a horse, a bit, harness and trappings, a chariot. In Caesar's time the nobles of Gaul were still known as "knights", *equites*. It can now be taken as established that the new techniques for riding and controlling horses, of which the bit of Thraco-Cimmerian type provides evidence, came into use among the Celts from the late 8th century onwards. At the same time there appeared the long iron sword which was the horseman's weapon *par excellence*. Henceforth the horse was the privilege and distinctive mark of the noble warrior, whether he rode it himself or used it to draw his chariot (at first four-wheeled, later two-wheeled).

Regional Variants of the Hallstatt Culture

The Hallstatt culture was largely an alien intrusion into Celtic territory. Many of its features came from other countries, the Balkans or Etruria or northern Italy. Even within the Celtic domain the various provincial cultures became differentiated in ways which are sometimes difficult to explain, some of the elements in the mosaic showing puzzling affinities with no basis in geographical proximity.

The formation of the Hallstatt culture of Burgundy, with its Italic imports (ribbed cistae) and features derived from the Austro-Bavarian region, is no doubt relatively easy to understand. But how are we to explain the appearance in Belgium in the 7th century of the Court-Saint-Etienne culture, with its rich tombs belonging to horsemen with iron swords? The horses' bits are of Bavarian and Hungarian type; the long iron swords, on the other hand, are not copied from Oriental models but imitate the contemporary bronze swords of western Early Hallstatt. For the most part the pottery shows strong affinities with the pottery of the lower Rhine in the final stages of the Urnfield culture, although certain pieces are reminiscent of southern types.

More complex still is the culture of Mailhac (Grand Bassin cemeteries), still strongly imbued with Urnfield traditions but with Danubian and Balkan features and Italic and Iberian affinities. Odette and Jean Taffanel, who have recently discovered horsemen's tombs dating from the 7th or early 6th century B.C., are inclined to the view that this very variegated culture was built up round an alien aristocracy from the northern or eastern part of the Celtic domain, incorporating a variety of features according to the external relationships of the different groups of newcomers.

But what are we to make of the culture which produced the warriors' tombs of Sesto Calende and Ca Morta in northern Italy? It bears no relationship to earlier cultures based on the local pattern, a late facies of the Urnfield culture (Golasecca), but has affinities in Spain and Languedoc (Mailhac), the Venetic territory (Este), Etruria and the Celtic area north of the Alps (antenna swords). Some scholars

(Bertrand, Reinach, H. Hubert) have seen in this culture evidence for the arrival of a first wave of Gauls, who had established themselves north of the Po by the end of the 7th century.

The date of the Sesto Calende tombs, which Italian archaeologists had put much too late, has recently been firmly established by the discovery at Corno Lauzo, near Mailhac, of a tomb containing weapons very similar to those found at Sesto Calende. The true date, attested by an Attic and an Ionian cup, is now known to be the middle of the 6th century B.C. There is no room for doubt about the aristocratic character of the Sesto Calende tombs: their furnishings included parts of two-wheeled chariots of Illyrian type together with horse-bits. The bits are of a later type than those found at Court-Saint-Etienne, resembling the type depicted on Illyrian and Venetic situlas of the 6th century B.C.

Then there is the extraordinary Jogassian-Vixian culture, now well known as a result of the work of Canon Favret, Lagorgette and R. Joffroy. It appears in Champagne at the end of the 6th century, and seems to be an intrusion from outside the area grafted on to a culture belonging to the final Urnfield stage. Some of its most characteristic objects, like the fibula *à fausse corde à bouclettes* to which Joffroy devotes so much attention, are widely distributed throughout Celtic territory. The long rapier with kidney-shaped decoration on the hilt is found over a wide area from southern Germany to Mailhac. The hollow torc and the dagger are represented on the statue found at Hirschlanden (Württemberg) depicting a heroised Celtic warrior of the late 6th century B.C. *(Plates 13, 14).*

The pottery, of which there are two purely local varieties (Les Jogasses and Vix), is extremely variegated. While the Jogasses ware shows some affinities with the pottery of Court-Saint-Etienne and the Urnfield sites of the lower Rhine on the one hand and the pottery of southern France on the other, the Vix ware has unexpected links with the Iberian world and northern Italy (Sesto Calende, Este, Villanova).

Finally there is the most recently discovered Hallstatt regional culture, that of Le Pègue, about which current excavations are yielding further evidence. This shows striking affinities with the cultures of Les Jogasses, Spain, Languedoc and northern Italy.

How, then, are we to explain the appearance in these various areas—Court-Saint-Etienne, Mailhac, Sesto Calende, Vix-les-Jogasses and Le Pègue—of such diverse cultures, linked by connections which are sometimes so difficult to explain and apparently formed round an aristocratic caste of horsemen or chariot-riders?

It may be possible to suggest an explanation if we consider a historical parallel. The evidence we have been discussing may well remind us of events in Europe at the end of the Middle Ages, when Flanders, the Low Countries and Burgundy, although forming part of the same political bloc, the "common market" built up under the powerful feudal authority of the Dukes of Burgundy, nevertheless maintained regular relationships with Spain and the Empire. And the numerous contacts between Burgundy and Flanders at that time would appear quite inexplicable if we were ignorant of the historical reasons for them.

Almost certainly there lies behind the mosaic of Hallstatt cultures, often showing close resemblances which at first sight are inexplicable, a historical reality which escapes us but which we can perhaps dimly apprehend from the comparison with other periods nearer to us and better known. The key to this system of cultural relationships probably lies in the horsemen's tombs, the "chariot tombs", attesting the existence of the aristocracy which was their driving force. May it be that some great princely family, which originally had connections with the Thraco-Cimmerian world and family links with the chiefs of the Celtic tribes in Bavaria, settled in northern Gaul and from there extended its influence to Languedoc, northern Italy and, at a later stage, Burgundy and Champagne? Thus a series of principalities would be established, maintaining close family ties with one another and consolidating cultural and trading relationships by a succession of marriages, alliances and personal unions.

Theories of this kind cannot, of course, be confirmed in detail. But, in broad terms, the realities concealed behind the archaeological evidence must inevitably be along these lines. We must regret that no Herodotus has recorded for us the story of these happenings, which we can dimly perceive must have taken place, although the details are beyond our ken. It is to be hoped that one of these days some new discovery will throw fresh light on these uncertainties.

The Celts and the Mediterranean

In addition to the factors we have been discussing there was another element which contributed to the formation of the regional cultures of the First Iron Age —the trading connections between the Celts and the more civilised peoples of the

Mediterranean basin. These connections were already known to the scholars of an earlier generation (Déchelette, Reinecke), but a flood of fresh light has been thrown on them by the new discoveries which have followed one another in such rapid succession in recent years. It is becoming increasingly clear that these trading links began at a very early period, that the form they took and the routes they followed varied from time to time, but that at certain periods they were much closer and more fruitful than might have been supposed.

In fact this trade began at a very early date, at the end of the 8th century. Evidence has been found in Alsace of economic relationships between northern Italy and the upper Rhine valley by way of the Alpine passes, in the form of the small pottery vases, imitating Villanovan types in bronze, discovered at Ensisheim (Haut-Rhin). They belong to the final phase of Late Bronze III (c. 750 B.C.). A Villanovan razor of the same period, dating from the end of the 8th century, was found in a tumulus in the Forêt de la Harth, between Colmar and Mulhouse. For the beginning of the 7th century we have the evidence of the Villanovan or Etruscan situlas from warrior tombs of the Hallstatt period in Burgundy.

But it is mainly on the Middle Hallstatt period (650–550 B.C.) that recent discoveries have thrown fresh light, sometimes of an entirely unexpected kind. At Saint-Blaise *(Plate 8)* H. Rolland discovered in Level VII abundant remains of wine amphoras and an extraordinary quantity of 7th century Etruscan black bucchero, together with fragments of Italo-Corinthian and Rhodian cups and vases of the same period. These articles, imported in the course of trade, are associated with remains of dwellings built on substantial foundations of pebbles, which point to a cultural influence stronger than might result from mere trading contacts; and this is confirmed by a sherd of native pottery on which are scratched five alphabetic characters. The evidence suggests, indeed, that even in this early period there was a settlement of urban type surrounded by a primitive defensive wall, parts of which were later built into the Greek ramparts. Thus the latest excavations have revealed the existence at Saint-Blaise of an important market town, an Etruscan trading post in contact with the merchants of Rhodes, as early as the end of the 7th century—i.e., before the foundation of Marseilles.

Further evidence has been provided by the very important Middle Hallstatt cemetery discovered near Pézenas by Canon Giry, which yielded *kantharoi* of black bucchero and Rhodian pottery in association with antenna daggers, fibulas and belt buckles dating from the second half of the 7th century. This cemetery, containing over six hundred tombs, threw valuable light both on the pattern of Mediterranean trade and on the chronology of the Hallstatt period in Languedoc. There seems to have been a whole chain of entrepôts extending up the Hérault valley from the site of Agde and the coastal area, with the object of directing the trade along this route. The Greek and Etruscan prospectors who visited this area were probably in quest of the copper and tin ore of the Montagne Noire.

To this period, when Mediterranean influence was beginning to reach into southern Gaul, belong a number of imported objects found in Gallic tombs to the north of the Alps—e.g., the ivory sphinx from Klein Aspergle in Württemberg and the Etruscan bronze pyxis found by M. Jehl and C. Bonnet in a tumulus in the Kasten-wald near Appenwihr (Haut-Rhin) *(Plates 11, 12)*. The lid of this remarkable piece, which has recently been restored in the laboratory of the Mainz museum, has been found to be decorated with repoussé figures of sphinxes. The bronze oenochoes of Rhodian origin found at Vilsingen, Kappel am Rhein and Le Pertuis probably belong to the same period.

In addition to these regular contacts between the Celtic world and the Mediter-ranean, first by way of the Alpine passes and later along the valleys of the Rhône and the Saône, there was also an inland trading route to the Danube valley, as well as a long-distance route, used as early as the 7th century B.C., which linked the Balkans, Italy and the eastern Mediterranean with Britain, taking the land route through Italy. A recent study by Christopher Hawkes has drawn attention to the importance of this last route, attested by the importation into Britain of bronze vessels (cauldrons and situlas) from Etruria and the Illyrian countries. During the Middle Hallstatt period these vessels were imitated in south-western Gaul and Armorica. The routes between the coast of Languedoc and Britain were probably the earliest routes for the importation of tin, one of the metals most sought after by the Mediterranean peoples.

From the beginning of the 6th century most of this trade with the Mediterranean seems to have passed through Marseilles and followed routes linking the various *oppida* on the hills dominating the Rhône and Saône valleys. At about the latitude of Lyons the roads divided, some running east, the others west. So active was the trade, however, that routes through the Alps and along the Danube valley were also in use. The tripod and *lebes* of Sainte-Colombe, imported from Cumae, are dated by Villard to the beginning of the 6th century, like the hydria found at Grächwyl, near Berne in Switzerland.

About 550 B.C., too, there was built on the Heuneburg, in the upper Danube valley, a great circuit of fortifications of Hellenic type, with a foundation of dressed stone supporting walls of mud brick. The technique of construction was Hellenic and typically Mediterranean. Clearly, therefore, there were much closer links between Greeks and Celts at this period than had been suspected. This was also the time when Mont Lassois reached its apogee: the oldest fragments of Attic vases discovered on this *oppidum* date, in Villard's opinion, from about 540 B.C.

The Tomb of Vix and the Excavations at Le Pègue

From the middle of the 6th century relations between Celts and Greeks developed considerably and fell into a regular and well ordered pattern. They were organised by the great feudal lords of the Seine, Saône, Rhine and Danube valleys. May we suppose that treaties had been entered into with Marseilles and other Greek cities, that there had been exchanges of diplomatic gifts? Behind this intense economic activity, hitherto barely suspected but now being revealed by excavation, we can see at work the same aristocratic caste of powerful feudal lords, now operating on an international scale. This was one of the revelations of the tomb of Vix. Although of exceptional quality, however, this tomb is by no means an isolated case, but takes its place among a considerable body of evidence belonging to the same period. The princely residence of Vix, on Mont Lassois, is comparable in all respects with those on the Heuneburg in the upper Danube valley, at Château-sur-Salins in the Jura and elsewhere. It is one of a series of entrepôts and fortified markets dominated by local dynasts controlling important trade routes.

A recent study by F. Bourriot in the *Revue Historique* (October-December 1965, pp. 285–310) stresses the religious character of the Vix burial. He suggests that the *krater* (mixing jar) found in the tomb was intended to hold libations of blood from ritual sacrifices similar to the human sacrifices mentioned by Strabo in his account of the Cimbri, which were carried out by priestesses over huge bronze vessels *(Plates 15, 16)*. Without accepting every detail of this attractive theory, it can readily be agreed that the Princess of Vix was also a priestess. We can find another proof of this in the two necklaces which accompanied her into the tomb —the open gold necklace with amber and diorite beads hanging from the front and the closed bronze necklace which originally had a leather band wound round it in a spiral. One of the two was a precious object, a personal possession which indicated the Princess's rank; the other was a liturgical object, the token of her priestly function. Another woman's tomb containing two necklaces has recently been found in the La Tène I a cemetery at Villeneuve-Renneville, which is thought to date from the 5th century B.C.

As for the decoration of the *krater* itself—a procession of warriors round Artemis, the patroness of young heroes—it seems probable that in the eyes of the Gauls it represented a cavalcade of warriors in honour of a native goddess *(Plate 18)*. It may be noted that the statuette of Artemis did not form part of the structure of the jar itself.

It sometimes happens that spectacular discoveries like the Vix burial raise more problems than they solve; indeed they might remain completely enigmatic but for the patient research and meticulous study of detail which make it possible to determine their historical setting. No doubt we can look to stratigraphic excavation of the *oppida* of the Hallstatt period, from the Danube valley to the Rhine, and to comparisons between these various stratigraphies, for answers to the problems raised by this important period, during which western Europe was brought within the ambit of the civilised world by the contact which it now established with the Mediterranean countries in the south. It may be hoped, for example, that the excavations at Le Pègue by the present author in association with A. Perraud and C. Lagrand will enlarge our understanding of the situation in this period, which is turning out to be more complicated than it appeared at the start of the enquiry. Each of the market settlements established by the native peoples for the purposes of trade is a microcosm in which are reflected all the vicissitudes to which the communities of Gaul were exposed.

The *oppidum* of Le Pègue *(Plates 9, 10)* was first occupied by a Ligurian tribe at the end of the Bronze Age and the beginning of the Iron Age. Terraces were laid out and hearths were constructed on the edge of the hill. The pottery found in this level is a ware in the Urnfield tradition belonging to the Early Hallstatt period. During the second half of the Late Hallstatt phase (end of 6th century B.C.) a group of dwellings was built in dry-stone and daub on a paved floor. The excavations of the last three years have made it possible to recover the plan of one of these dwellings, in the form of a square 8 metres each way with partitions dividing it into three rooms. This level yielded imported pottery—Attic black-figure vases, grey Phocaean ware from Marseilles and Massiliote amphoras. The most interesting feature, which indicates the strength of Hellenic influences on the regional cultures in this period, is a "pseudo-Ionian" type of pottery, showing a technique and shapes which are Greek (originally from Asia Minor) and decorative patterns which are sometimes Greek and sometimes indigenous Hallstatt. Evidence is accumulating that this pottery is of regional manufacture, some of it perhaps even locally produced. In addition the native pottery is itself often influenced by Greek models, and is found imitating the shapes of imported vases. At the very end of the 6th century there was constructed within this settlement, which had undergone much alteration and was partly destroyed, a grain store consisting of a number of small compartments built in daub, within which jars of light earthenware were set out in rows. In this level appears a new type of Hallstatt pottery, not manufactured in the area and showing affinities in shape and decoration with the pottery of Les Jogasses in Champagne. The grain store was destroyed by fire about 500 B.C. Trial trenching recently carried out near the school at Le Pègue has shown that by this period a small Gallic community had established itself near the river. Later, at the beginning of the 4th century, a new settlement seems to have been built on the hill. The level corresponding to this second establishment was much disturbed by later terracing. The 4th century level, revealed in the excavations near the school, contains a number of characteristic objects—a fibula, pottery, fire-dogs with rams' heads. At the end of the 4th century there seems to have been a good deal of constructional work, dated by pottery from Magna Graecia ("Pre-Gnathia"), but this does not seem to have led to the establishment of a permanent settlement. Meanwhile, at the same period, the Gallic village in the valley was still occupied; it was apparently fortified soon afterwards, in La Tène II. It was also during this period and in La Tène III (2nd century B.C.) that settlers began to return in some numbers to the hill, which now took on the appearance of a small Celto-Ligurian township. Remains of various community services which have been observed (an approach road hewn from the rock, a water conduit probably drawing a supply from a nearby spring) appear to date from this period.

Comparative Stratigraphy of the Oppida

The site at Le Pègue is of outstanding interest for the light it throws on the developing influence of the Mediterranean peoples at the end of the 6th century and on the history of the Celtic world and events in the Rhine valley between the 6th and 1st century B.C. A comparison between the stratigraphy of Le Pègue, Malpas in the Ardèche and the Heuneburg in the upper Danube valley brings out certain fundamental elements common to all three which open up interesting historical vistas.

1. These fortified Hallstatt sites almost always date from the end of the Bronze Age or the beginning of the Iron Age (between 900 and 700 B.C.).

2. On the upper Danube, as in the Rhône valley, the second half of the 6th century was marked by intense economic activity and by the apogee of relations with the Mediterranean. Fortifications were built, market centres were established, and Greek imports and the cultural influences they brought with them reached their peak.

3. This period of euphoria was followed by a crisis, the beginnings of which were felt on the upper Danube about 520 B.C., and which burst on the Rhône valley about 500. The settlements were burned down, the fortifications razed to the ground and the stocks of goods in the entrepôts destroyed. The likeliest explanation for these devastations is that they were caused by the arrival of a first body of Celts coming from the Danube valley, the Rhine and eastern France and heading for northern Italy. In the light of the archaeological evidence Livy's references to the migrations of the Gauls take on enhanced value and significance—in particular the passage describing how the tribes led by Bellovesus were held up for some time in the Tricastin area before finding a route through the mountains to their objective in northern Italy (Livy, *History of Rome*, V, 34). It is true that Livy assigns too early a date to this first Gallic invasion, which he makes contemporary with the reign of Tarquin the Elder and the foundation of Marseilles, but we can readily establish the correct date from the fact that when the Gauls arrived in the Po valley they came into conflict with the Etruscans; and we know that the arrival of the Etruscans in this area was not earlier than the end of the 6th century (capture of Felsina/Bologna, 525 B.C.).

Strangely, this invasion, as it is recorded in the stratigraphic data, seems to have been preceded by a period of bustling activity among the Celtic tribes, some of them moving north and others south; these movements had no warlike purpose but were probably connected with the development of trading relations with the Mediterranean. Thus in Champagne we find the Jogassian culture centred on an intrusive element with Mediterranean affinities; and the occurrence of Jogassian features at Le Pègue about 500 B.C. can be explained only by influences from the north.

However this may be, the first wave of Gallic invaders making for northern Italy seems to have claimed one major casualty—the trading route with its network of entrepôts which ran from Marseilles by way of the Rhône and Saône valleys to link the Mediterranean with the Celtic world. The whole system of trading exchanges and marketing arrangements was temporarily destroyed. Accordingly on the sites of almost all the native settlements, as well as at Marseilles and Saint-Blaise, the 5th century is a complete blank; and the distribution of Etruscan products in the 5th century shows that trade now passed through the Alps from Etruscan ports on the Adriatic like Spina into the Rhine and Moselle valleys.

4. There were signs of recovery at the beginning of the 4th century, but this soon suffered a setback with the arrival of a fresh wave of Gallic invaders. This invasion, contemporary with the capture of Rome, is historically well attested (Livy, V, 35 ff.).

This is as far as we can go on the evidence of comparative stratigraphy; but the study of the site at Le Pègue also yields information about other matters as well —on the one hand the re-establishment of Massiliote influence from the end of the 4th century onwards, on the other the process of steady fusion between the Celts and the Ligurians during the 3rd and 2nd centuries B.C.

The Formation of the La Tène Culture

The emergence of the La Tène culture, which appeared just as the Hallstatt culture was flickering into extinction, presents us with a most baffling and perplexing problem. Between 500 and 480 B.C.—the period of the Princess of Vix—a very distinctive culture appeared farther to the north, in the area between the Meuse and the Main and Neckar valleys. This entirely new and individual culture had connections with the Eurasian world farther to the east and with the Mediterranean civilisations, but nevertheless remained completely independent. As the La Tène culture, its influence was to spread far and wide. Its emergence and development were rapid, brilliant and unexpected. The area in which it was formed lay to the north of the centre of gravity of the final Hallstatt phase, in the valleys of the Marne, the Meuse, the Moselle, the middle Rhine, the Main and the Neckar. It must be admitted that at the beginning of the 5th century we cannot mark out any precise geographical boundary between the areas in which the Early La Tène culture was already active and those in which Late Hallstatt still survived. In the Marne valley, one of the first areas to be affected by the new culture, there were still Jogassian pockets. The culture seems to have varied with the different tribes, and these had not yet settled down in their permanent homes. Even within the Moselle and Rhine valleys there were areas which remained unaffected by the new trends, like the Ardennes and the Rhine slate plateau (the Hunsrück-Eifel region). This period, indeed, is an outstanding example of the way in which different cultures can live side by side in self-contained compartments.

We may now try to identify the political, social and economic circumstances which favoured the emergence of the distinctive La Tène culture.

When we compare the Celtic world as we know it at the beginning of the La Tène period with the aristocratic cultures of the First Iron Age we observe both similarities and differences. In the earliest phase of La Tène there is still an aristocracy enriched by trade with the Mediterranean countries, whose presence is attested by the princely tombs of southern Germany—Schwarzenbach, Rodenbach, Dürkheim, Armsheim, Weisskirchen, Klein Aspergle and so on. The tombs of this period, however, are different in some respects from those of the earlier period. They contain mainly Etruscan objects, associated with very handsome native-made ornaments imitated from Greco-Scythian models. We have already noted that the pattern of markets had changed and that new trading routes were now being used. The trade was no longer in the hands of the Greeks but of the Etruscans, and the influence of the Eurasian world to the east was now more strongly felt, being transmitted by the Scythians who had invaded Central Europe in the 6th century and were now reaching out towards the Danube.

There was another factor at work, perhaps one of still greater importance. The chalk plateaux of the Paris basin and the heavy soil of Picardy, lying to the west of the main area of concentration of the princely tombs of La Tène, were now being settled by a considerable population of Celtic farmers. The large La Tène cemeteries in Champagne, Brie and the Aisne valley give us a quite new picture of Gallic society. Side by side with an aristocracy riding in two-wheeled chariots, more numerous than in the earlier period, we find a prosperous peasantry and a considerable class of craftsmen. The general impression is of a sharp growth in population, a fair degree of economic wellbeing and a reasonably high technological and cultural level.

Moreover the 5th century seems to have seen a transformation in farming methods associated with the introduction of improved equipment and the general progress of society. The farmers of the First Iron Age preferred the light soils of the hill-sides and plateaux; those of the La Tène period brought the heavy soil of the valleys into cultivation. They were able to do this because in place of a light wooden plough which merely scratched the surface they used a heavy plough with an iron share, with which they were able to draw deep parallel furrows and secure effective drainage of the soil. This period, too, saw the appearance of cultivated meadows, the grass in which could be cut with an iron scythe, making it possible to build up stocks of hay and thus improve the efficiency and productivity of cattle-rearing. The Gallic expansion had as a direct consequence the invasions of northern Italy, where, as we have already noted, excavation has made it possible to establish an accurate chronology. The recent discoveries by Italian archaeologists to the south of Bologna—in particular the 5th century black-figure *kylix* found in a La Tène cemetery of Gallic type (cf. G. A. Mansuelli, "Problemi storici della civiltà gallica in Italia", in *Hommages à Albert Grenier*, vol. III, p. 1077) and fibulas of La Tène I a type (5th century) found on the Etruscan site of Marzabotto—indicate that the Celts were established in northern Italy by the 5th century.

The Arnoaldi situla *(Plates 26, 27)*, which cannot be exactly dated but must be earlier than the second wave of Celtic invasions, shows a group of Celtic infantry-men, wearing Illyrian helmets and carrying the oblong Gallic shield with its characteristic *umbo*, together with some Etruscan soldiers, all forming part of the same troop. Thus suggests that the first Celtic tribes to settle in northern Italy achieved a peaceful symbiosis with the Etruscans; and no doubt it was this ami-cable relationship which enabled commercial contacts to be resumed on a new basis during the 5th century. But the second wave of Gallic invasions, beginning with the capture of Rome and ending with the destruction of the Etruscan city of Melpum—thereafter replaced by the Gallic settlement of Bologna—seems to have dealt a severe blow to imports of Mediterranean goods into the countries north of the Alps. The latest known object of this kind is the Waldalgesheim situla, an import from southern Italy dated to the middle of the 4th century; after this date luxury vases of Mediterranean origin disappear from the tombs.

On the other hand relations with the Scythians and Iranians to the east intensified during the 4th century. The tomb of Trichtingen in Württemberg yielded a silver torc terminating in two protomes of bulls, probably imported from Persia *(Plate 23)*. It was at this period that the Celts established themselves in the Balkans and sent an embassy to Alexander the Great; at a later date they were to found independent kingdoms in Asia Minor.

At the end of the 4th century a further change took place. Recent excavations in Provence (Glanum, Saint-Blaise) and Languedoc (Ensérune) have revealed that there was a fresh burst of urban settlement at this period, apparently associated with a revival of Massiliote influence. This was also the time when the Massiliote navigator Pytheas sailed on his voyage of exploration into northern seas—as we have recently been reminded by the discovery of a gold coin of this period on a beach in Brittany. It was probably at this period, too, that Marseilles took advantage of the difficulties its main rival, Carthage, was encountering in Spain and the Mediterranean to reorganise the traffic in British tin, very profitably for itself, so that traders' caravans passed through Gaul. In general, however, the merchants of Marseilles no longer dealt to any considerable extent in luxury goods but were mainly concerned with the transport of wine and Campanian pottery.

Summary

After the decline of the Urnfield culture in the 8th century B.C. the Celtic world was dominated by two successive types of culture—in the First Iron Age the Hallstatt culture and in the Second Iron Age the La Tène culture. The radical differences between the two have not always been sufficiently stressed. The Hallstatt culture was, in origin, alien to the Celts, heterogeneous, divided into numerous provincial variants; the La Tène culture was from the beginning homogeneous, national and with the capacity for expansion.

The processes by which the various regional Hallstatt cultures became differentiated from one another raises problems which in the present state of knowledge cannot readily be solved. As a working hypothesis, however, it may be supposed that a number of powerful noble families founded dynasties and established principalities, which might sometimes have outlying fiefs, just as in the great feudal estates of the Middle Ages. This is the only plausible explanation for the puzzling affinities sometimes found between these cultures—for example the links of Mailhac with Spain and Bavaria, of Sesto Calende with Illyria and Languedoc, of Le Pègue with Vix-les-Jogasses. Another factor leading to differentiation and to links with other areas lay in the development of relationships between the Celts and the peoples of the Mediterranean countries (Villanova, Etruria, Greece) which had begun as early as the 8th century B.C.

At the time when their economic and cultura connections with the Celtic world were at a peak the Greeks, with the help of the native peoples themselves, seem to have set out to look for new trade routes, along which there soon grew up a series of trading posts organised by the native tribes. Such entrepôts as those at Mont Lassois, the Heuneburg and Le Pègue seem to have been founded by tribes who were in effect specialising in this trade. The various establishments in this quite highly organised network would be controlled by powerful dynasts, like those who ruled from the Heuneburg or Vix-Sainte-Colombe.

Comparison of the stratigraphy of the Heuneburg; Malpas and Le Pègue suggests that there was a wave of destruction and burning about 500 B.C., which can be related to the first wave of Gallic invaders making for northern Italy. The date assigned to this invation in a well known passage in Livy (600 B.C.) is too early, and it can now be put at about 500 B.C. on the basis of finds at these *oppida* and in 5th century Gallic tombs excavated at Casiola Valsenio, south of Bologna.

To this Gallic invasion of 500 B.C. and its consequences—the destruction of the network of trading posts in the Rhône and Saône valleys and the Jura and the establishment of Gallic settlements in Cisalpine Gaul—can be attributed the profound changes which took place after this date in the pattern of trade between the Mediterranean countries and the Celtic world. Spina now supplanted Marseilles, and the routes through the Alpine passes superseded the roads along the valleys of the Rhône and the Seine.

The fact remains, however, that the creation by the Celts in the 5th century of a national culture and a distinctive art of their own is still, in large measure, difficult to explain. Does it become any easier to understand if we observe that it took place during a period of demographic expansion, of technological progress, particularly in agriculture, and of a rising standard of living, and if we suppose that this dynamic people, organised round its kings and chieftains, was now beginning to become conscious of its own potentialities? Then, when it set out on the conquest of southern and eastern Europe, there grew up within this people a kind of national unity, based on a community of language, culture and religious traditions, in spite of their high degree of political fragmentation. Thus if the Hallstatt period can be considered as the age of princes and great feudal lords perhaps we may regard the 5th and later centuries as the age of the Celtic nation.

The second wave of Gallic invaders at the beginning of the 4th century, however, broke the truce with the Etruscans and once again disturbed the regular connections with the Mediterranean world. After 350 B.C., following their drive towards the Balkans, the Celts tended instead to establish contact with the Scythians by way of neighbouring peoples. Then from the end of the 4th century onwards the resumption of Massiliote expansion led to the development of urban settlement in southern Gaul and made it possible to re-establish the age-old contacts between the Celts and the Mediterranean.

THE LA TÈNE CULTURE

IV

W e must now give some general account of the La Tène culture, the basis of the native Gallic culture which was a distinctive component in the provincial cultures of Gaul under the Roman Empire. The chronology of La Tène, first sketched out by O. Tischler, has been steadily developed and refined by the work of Reinecke and Viollier, followed by Jacobsthal's excellent study of Celtic art and more recently by O. Klindt-Jensen.

Chronology and Typology

Tischler's classification, the broad lines of which are still valid, was based on changes in the form of fibulas. The foot of the La Tène I fibula stands clear of the bow, terminating either in a thickened end or in a stud of coral. In La Tène II the foot is joined to the bow but is still vestigially represented by a slight annular or globular swelling. In La Tène III this swelling disappears and the catchplate is simplified and takes on a trapezoidal form. The form of the sword, its scabbard and the chape on the end of the scabbard also go through a process of evolution. In La Tène I the sword is pointed and relatively short, and the scabbard ends in an openwork chape. In La Tène II the sword is longer and the chape is no longer openwork. In La Tène III the sword is very long, with a rounded end; the scabbard is of similar shape and is decorated with a ladder-like pattern of small strips of metal.

At the beginning of the 20th century Reinecke was able, on the basis of the rich furnishings of the *Fürstengräber* or princely tombs of southern Germany, to distinguish an additional phase in the chronological succession, associated with fairly heavy fibulas with an S-shaped bow, decorated with stylised birds or anthropoid masks. He called this first period La Tène A and the others La Tène B, C and D.

Later the Swiss scholar Viollier, in a systematic study of the cemeteries on the Swiss plateau, distinguished several subdivisions in Tischler's La Tène I. He recognised, first, a phase which he called La Tène I a, characterised by fibulas with a semicircular bow, an elongated foot standing well clear of the bow, and a voluminous spring; this phase, corresponding broadly to Reinecke's La Tène A (5th century B.C.), was not, in Viollier's view, represented in northern Italy. In La Tène I b the fibulas have a flattened bow, sometimes indeed of violin-bow shape, which is frequently thickened and decorated; the foot is shorter and is often decorated with a stud of coral; and the spring becomes less prominent. In La Tène I c the bow becomes shorter and broader, while the foot is longer and ends in a conical boss.

As a result of the work of Jacobsthal and Klindt-Jensen it has been possible to relate these new subdivisions to the successive styles of Gallic art, producing the following scheme:

La Tène I a (c. 480–400 B.C.): Jacobsthal's "Early Celtic", a flamboyant style based on the Greek palmette.

La Tène I b (c. 400–350 B.C.): a fantastic style showing the influence of Scythian art.

La Tène I c (c. 350–250 B.C.): Jacobsthal's "Waldalgesheim style", a purely Celtic style; later the beginning of Jacobsthal's "plastic style".

La Tène II   (c. 250–120 B.C.): Jacobsthal's "plastic style" and "sword style".

La Tène III (120–50 B.C.): the style found at Entremont and on the Gundestrup cauldron.

The Styles of Ornamental Art

The distinctive character of Celtic art lies mainly in the fact that, having originally been concerned principally with the production of ornaments in gold and other metals, it retained a visible predilection for graphic effects and a predominant tendency towards stylisation, always with something of the spirit and the techniques of the metalworking crafts.

The first style of Celtic art, whose period of vogue seems to correspond roughly with the 5th century B.C. (La Tène I a), is still fairly close to Greek and Etruscan models. It uses a modified version of the Greek palmette, treating it in a flamboyant manner but still with a measure of classical restraint. The most characteristic examples of this style are a gold torc from Besseringen, a gold torc and bracelet from the Reinheim tomb, a gold necklace and a dish with gold openwork decoration from Schwarzenbach, and a gold necklace from Dürkheim.

In the 4th century (La Tène I b) appears a fantastic style much more strongly influenced by Scythian art. The best specimens of this style are the decoration of the oenochoes from Basse-Yutz now in the British Museum *(Plates 21, 22)*, a bronze clasp from Weisskirchen decorated with coloured enamels, a gold necklace from Rodenbach *(Plate 29)*, and the Erstfelden gold torcs and bracelets, recently discovered in the Swiss canton of Uri, on the St Gotthard road.

After this period of Baroque exuberance, which seems to have lasted throughout the first half of the 4th century (Viollier's La Tène I b), there appears what Jacobsthal calls the "Waldalgesheim style". The best examples of this style, spare and restrained in comparison with its predecessor, are a torc and bracelet from Waldalgesheim, a gold torc from Filottrano *(Plate 28)* and the Hallein oenochoe *(Plates 24, 25)*. The Greek palmette is now transposed into a series of curvilinear motifs—circles, stars and double S's—constituting a whole new grammar of ornament which diverges widely from earlier models. The development of this new style can be related to Viollier's La Tène I c (late 4th and early 3rd century B.C.).

In the 3rd century a new style emerged, more concerned with three-dimensional effect—Jacobsthal's "plastic style". This is characterised by an interest in sharp reliefs, a systematic exploitation of light and shade. The most typical products of this period, well studied by Klindt-Jensen, are the Brå cauldron *(Plate 63)* and the openwork plastic decoration of Malomeriče.

At the end of the 3rd and beginning of the 2nd century Celtic ornamental art is represented mainly by the rich engraved decoration of the La Tène II swords, which has recently been studied by J. M. de Navarro. This style has a rich repertoire of ornament, with borrowings from Scythian and Iranian art contributing to an exuberant range of decorative motifs which diverge ever more widely from their models.

Finally the 1st century is dominated by the primitive, archaic and pre-realist style of the Gundestrup cauldron *(Plates 48–60)*. This silver vessel with decorative panels in repoussé work, one of the major achievements of Gallic art, was discovered in a Danish bog in 1880. The equipment of the warriors depicted on the cauldron belongs to the La Tène III period, and the religious beliefs to which it gives expression have close parallels in Gallo-Roman iconography, particularly of the early 1st century. It seems likely that the cauldron was produced in northern or eastern Gaul and brought with them by fugitives from Roman power.

The Development of Sculpture

It is a matter of some difficulty to establish synchronisms between the development of Gallic sculpture and of ornamental art. No works of sculpture have yet been identified as dating from the earliest period (5th century)—though this does not, of course, mean that no sculpture was produced during this period.

The carved stone pillar from Pfalzfeld (*Kreis* of St Goar) *(Plate 38)*, now in the Bonn Museum, seems to derive from the Waldalgesheim style (4th century). So also does the statue of a warrior from Grézan, which can be dated by the belt buckle with four prongs, of a type similar to a buckle recently found by Odette and Jean Taffanel in a 4th century tomb at Mailhac.

A date at the end of the 3rd century seems likely for the squatting figures and janus heads of Roquepertuse *(Plates 41–43)*, the expressionism and hieratic postures of which may mark the highest point of the purely Gallic style, associated with the fusion between Celts and Ligurians in the Rhône valley.

The statuary of Entremont, already strongly imbued with Roman influences, belongs to the end of the 2nd or beginning of the 1st century B.C. It cannot be asserted with confidence that all this work dates from before the Roman conquest: it is significant, for example, that a woman's head found at Entremont shows the same hair style, with plaits wound round the head in a kind of diadem, as a funerary portrait of Republican date from Nîmes.

The "*tarasque*" or monster of Noves *(Plates 46, 47)*, in a style which shows strong affinities with the Gundestrup cauldron, seems to date from the 1st century B.C. The distinctive individuality of Gallic art depends partly on its persistent concern with graphic stylisation and partly on the expressionism which gives its figures of animals, human beings and gods a fantastic and obsessional character. This art stands at the opposite extreme from the humanism and rationalism of the Greeks and Romans. The Gallic artist, totally possessed by his sense of mystery and the supernatural, seeks to ward off the effects of divine power by a kind of magic of idols and symbols, and tends to conceive divinity in the most haunting, fantastic and hideous forms. Nevertheless we sense in the development of this art from the 5th to the 1st century B.C. an irresistible urge towards realism and anthropomorphism, under the combined influence of the Etruscans, the Greeks and later the Romans.

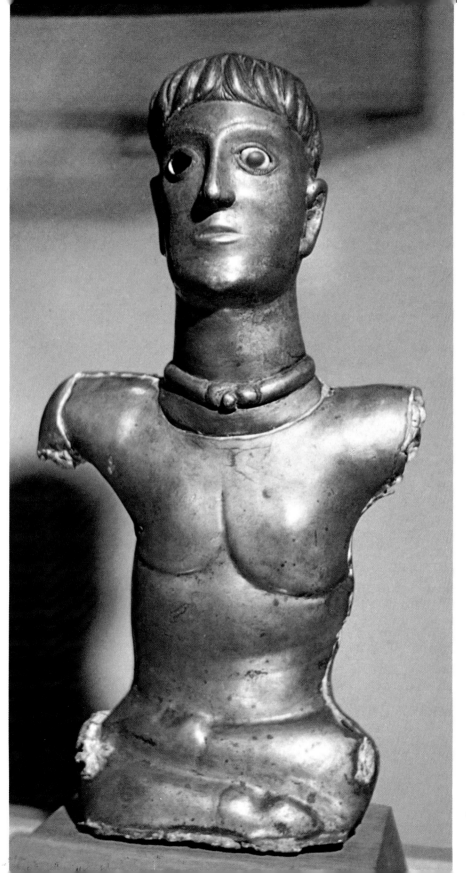

45

48, 49, 50 ↑

61

62

63

64

65

68

69

72

73

Metalworking Techniques

One dominant theme runs through all the artistic output of the Gauls—the feeling for craftmanship, with all that that implies in terms of technical expertise and delight in professional skills. The Gauls were craftsmen of outstanding quality. Starting with a readiness to learn from the technical skills of the Mediterranean world, they were soon able to develop their own industries along the same lines, modified to suit the different natural conditions and human environment of western Europe.

Ironworking rapidly developed into the basic industry of the Gauls. During the Second Iron Age (the La Tène period) it seems to have been practised everywhere, enabling every organised community to become self-sufficient, manufacturing its own implements and weapons. Recent investigations have shown that forging techniques developed considerably between the First and Second Iron Ages. After directing their efforts during the Hallstatt period towards obtaining the purest possible metal (which had certain disadvantages, for iron in the pure state is soft and malleable) the ironsmiths of Gaul learned by experience how to harden iron by hammering it and case-hardening it by contact with red-hot embers, and thus to obtain strips of mild iron which they welded together to make swords. Recent metallographic analyses by Lepage seem to show that this technique, which was to develop into the method of manufacturing swords of welded damascene steel practised in the period of the great invasions, was already used in an elementary form during the La Tène period.

Some of the products of the La Tène ironsmiths are remarkable for their extraordinary technical competence—in particular the scabbards of exceedingly thin sheet iron decorated with delicate engraved and repoussé ornament, or sometimes imitating the grain of leather with a pattern of delicate striations. Other striking examples of their skill are provided by the iron fibulas in the Troyes museum, which look as if they had been cast in moulds; but they are made of mild iron, the technique for casting which was not invented until two thousand four hundred years later. They seem in fact to have been produced by hot stamping rather than by casting in the normal sense of the term.

In the field of bronze-working the Gauls sought, with great ingenuity and resourcefulness, to counter the natural disadvantages resulting from the shortage of copper and particularly of tin in their territory. Gallic bronze has frequently a low tin content, the deficiency being sometimes made good by the addition of calamine, an ore containing a mixture of copper and zinc. The metal obtained by this means was brass, known as *orichalcum* to the ancients, who were not acquainted with zinc in the pure state. It was much used, particularly in the manufacture of fibulas, for which its ductility and elasticity made it very suitable.

The Gauls are credited by Pliny with inventing and practising the techniques of tinning and silvering by the use of mercury; and it is certainly true that tinned and silvered objects are commonly found in Gaul. Recent investigations by G. A. Duch have suggested that the Gauls used an ingenious technique for the distillation of mercury: this seems to have been the purpose of kilns discovered in recent excavations at Alesia, the distinctive feature of which is a large slab of limestone with spiral channels on the upper surface.

Enamel and Glass

The Gauls made use of enamel over a long period for decorating bronze, silver and even iron articles. The technique was well known to them during the period of independence, and developed considerably in Roman times. It was long believed that the bracelets moulded from coloured glass and decorated with net patterns in glass of different colours were trinkets imported from abroad; but the remains of glass-working shops recently discovered at Manching in Bavaria show that these articles were also made by the Celts themselves within their own territory.

The Art of Building

It used to be thought that the Gauls were ignorant of the art of building in stone. We now, however, have numerous remains of fortifications built either of stone or in a characteristic form of construction known as the *murus gallicus*, consisting of stone walls with a timber framing. Bersu's excavations on the Wittnauer Horn in Switzerland suggest that the origins of this building technique go back to the Hallstatt period. The later discoveries on the Heuneburg in the upper Danube valley allow us to follow the development of the technique in the 5th and 4th centuries B.C.; for after the mid 6th century mud-brick wall which has already been referred to the Celtic occupants of the Heuneburg built a wall of stone and timber construction—the oldest *murus gallicus* known—at the beginning of the La Tène period.

The exact date of the extraordinary fortifications on Mont Sainte-Odile in Alsace is not yet known with certainty, but the excavations by H. Zumstein in 1964–65–66 have shown that they are certainly earlier than the Roman period and probably later than the end of the Bronze Age. On present evidence the date is most likely to lie somewhere between the 8th and 4th centuries B.C. This immense structure, in which the stonework was originally bound together with splay-ended timber beams, is in many other respects—the arrangement of the gates and the use of wedge-shaped stones to maintain the horizontality of the courses on the slopes of the hill—reminiscent of the defensive walls of the Greek archaic period, when Greek influence on the Celtic world was at its height.

The Building of the Gallo-Greek Towns

As many observers have noted, as J. Jannoray demonstrated so clearly, and as Odette Taffanel has recently confirmed, the comparative stratigraphy of the Ligurian and Gallic *oppida* of southern France reveals three phases of town building—the first during the second half of the 6th century B.C., the second in the late 5th and early 4th century, and the third from the end of the 4th to the beginning of the 2nd century. With minor variations which are no doubt due to local circumstances, this clear-cut division into three phases separated by considerable gaps is found everywhere and is undoubtedly the result of far-reaching historical causes.

On the basis of the evidence now being provided by the excavations at Le Pègue —showing a Celtic presence in the Rhône valley in the 5th century B.C.—it seems plausible to relate these three phases of town building and the periods of inactivity between them to the alternation between the great waves of Gallic invaders and the successive revivals of Greek trade and the influence of the Mediterranean countries, mostly passing through Marseilles and reaching far into the interior of Gaul.

The first period of town building is clearly to be connected with the hellenisation of Gaul in the latter part of the 6th century by way of Marseilles and the Rhône valley. It came to an end when the first wave of Gallic invaders arrived at the end of the 6th and beginning of the 5th century: the first conflagration level at Le Pègue, with its evidence of wholesale destruction, seems to have its counterparts at Malpas, Roquemaure, Mailhac and even Ensérune. The second period is a relatively brief interlude, particularly well attested in Languedoc (Mailhac, Ensérune), between the troubled period around 500 B.C. which has recently been revealed by archaeology and the second wave of Gallic invasions, which is dated by historical evidence to the beginning of the 4th century B.C. The final phase of town building—the longest and most important—began at the end of the 4th century, when Marseilles was re-establishing its trading interests in Gaul, and continued into the 3rd and 2nd centuries. It may have suffered setbacks or interruptions in certain areas in the disturbed period which seems to have occurred at the end of the 4th century, with the arrival of Hannibal and his army, but on the evidence at present available it does not appear to have been affected by the Celtic drive through the whole of southern Gaul around the year 300 or by the Belgic invasions about 250 B.C.

The Archaeological Evidence

This alternation of peaceful and troubled periods undoubtedly played an important part in the changing pattern of Gallic culture. For the first phase we have still little information about the style of building in towns, either in the Mediterranean zone or within the main Celtic domain in eastern France and southern Germany. Until the last few years it seemed reasonable to suppose that the Celts of the Rhine and Danube valleys, like the Ligurians along the Mediterranean, had remained faithful to the traditional native type of settlement; but two recent discoveries—the finding at Le Pègue in 1964 of foundations and paving of well defined structure and regular orientation, and the excavation of buildings within the fortified area on the Heuneburg—have shown that even in this period the native peoples had begun to lay out regularly planned towns under the influence of archaic Greece. The composite cultures which produced the pseudo-Ionian pottery of Le Pègue and built the stone and brick defensive works and the quite elaborate timber dwellings on the Heuneburg bear witness to a profound interpenetration of barbarian and Mediterranean elements which is unexpected at such an early period.

In Jannoray's opinion the second phase is marked at Ensérune by the establishment of a real urban settlement in place of the original village. In the last quarter of the 5th century we find stone-built houses being erected on the hill, laid out on a grid plan within a defensive wall. For storage purposes the occupants abandoned the silo which had been common in the earlier period and used instead a *dolium* sunk into the floor of the house, apparently taking their cue from the Greek colonies in the West. What is, in Jannoray's view, almost more important is that "during the second period of the *oppidum* there was developed at Ensérune a provincial order of architecture which, though showing the Hellenic influences which pervaded the western Mediterranean, is nevertheless an original creation. It bears witness to a constant striving towards artistic achievement on the part of the inhabitants." Here Jannoray is referring to the distinctive local types of capital, showing the influence of the Doric and Ionic orders, surmounting the column which stood in the centre of the houses and supported the roof structure.

The numerous Iberian graffiti found at Ensérune show that this was the language spoken by the people of the town. The Celts had not yet arrived in any numbers, although from the end of the 5th century their influence can be detected in certain articles (clasps, fibulas) which reached the town in the course of trade.

The second period of town building is also represented at Mailhac by dwellings on a rectangular plan, perhaps rather less carefully built and less monumental in character than at Ensérune. But were the Gauls—who had probably reached Upper Provence and the Cévennes by this period—actually involved in this second town building phase in the 5th–4th centuries B.C.? In the present state of knowledge it is difficult to be sure. On the hill site at Le Pègue the levels belonging to this period have been almost completely destroyed by later reconstruction; and the most recent excavations (1961 to 1963) of the village in the plain, situated near a ford crossing the stream, suggest that it was of purely native type, built of wattle and daub on a dry-stone foundation. The excavations have not, however, covered a large enough area to reveal the layout of the whole settlement.

The third town building phase begins at the end of the 4th century and extends into the 3rd and 2nd. It is marked by a number of important historical developments:

1. the expansion of Marseilles, which after a long period during which it was no more than a small trading post on the Lacydon began in the 4th century to establish a series of colonies to the east and west, from Nice to Agde;

2. the advance of the Celts to the Mediterranean coast;

3. the establishment along the Languedoc coast of a number of Gallic princedoms, strongly influenced by Greece and maintaining trade relations with Marseilles and its colonies;

4. the coexistence of Celts and Ligurians in Provence, leading to a gradual assimilation between the two peoples and to the foundation of Celto-Ligurian *oppida* and sanctuaries (although, unlike the Celtiberians of Languedoc, the Celto-Ligurians of Upper Provence seem to have proved uncomfortable neighbours for Marseilles, retaining much of their savage and warlike disposition).

Although the assumed prototypes of native town building between the 6th and 4th centuries B.C. are still unknown, we have in Olbia, near Hyères, a Greek city founded by Marseilles at the end of the 4th century. The excavations by Coupry on this site during the last ten or twelve years have gradually been bringing to light the remains of its walls, its layout and the first traces of its sanctuaries. The fine Greek defensive walls of Saint-Blaise also belong to this phase, whatever the exact date to be assigned to them (4th or 3rd century B.C.?). Also of this period are the remains of Greek walls at Saint-Rémy, together with a small area of the ancient town in which, by some fortunate dispensation, there have survived a number of houses on a plan similar to those on Delos and the remains of a Hellenistic agora in which a temple to Cybele was erected at a later date.

Hellenistic Towns and Celto-Ligurian Oppida

Comparisons between coastal colonies like Olbia and Saint-Blaise, the hellenised cities of the interior like Glanum and Celtic *oppida* like Entremont, Nages, Orgon and Le Pègue are extremely instructive. Thus the Salyan city of Entremont *(Plates 39, 40)*, which F. Benoit believes to date from the beginning of the 3rd century B.C., appears—in spite of a certain regularity of plan—distinctly crude in comparison with the refinements, the elegance and the comfort found on earlier sites. This relatively barbarous quality is seen in the irregularities in the construction of the defensive walls, in the small size of the houses, the structure of which seems conditioned by the necessities of defence, and above all in the abundant material on Celtic art, religion and ritual which has been recovered in the excavations: such things as the skulls pierced by nails, bearing witness to the savage and repellent custom recorded by ancient authors of nailing human heads (either enemy trophies or relics of ancestors) on the fronts of houses and temples, religious representations of personages—either heroes or gods—sitting in a squatting posture with their hands resting on human heads, and lintels with cavities hollowed out to hold skulls. We feel ourselves transported into a barbarian world quite alien to the Hellenistic cities only a short distance away. No doubt the technique of sculpture, the general layout of the towns and the stone buildings show strong

Mediterranean influences. But the Greek and Etruscan contribution was of a purely technical character: it did not affect the essential substance of the Gauls' beliefs and rites, nor the national individuality of their art.

Benoit's assertion that all the religious beliefs and the whole of the ritual and iconography of the Gauls of the Rhône valley in the La Tène II and III periods are wholly derived from Mediterranean prototypes and from some common store *(koine)* of beliefs and customs shared by the peoples bordering on the Mediterranean is surely an overstatement, based on a misunderstanding of the historical background of this third phase of Gallo-Greek culture, during which the Celto-Ligurians, subject though they might be to Etruscan and Greek influences, nevertheless gave expression to their national personality with a dynamism of which the Hellenistic cities were the first to feel the effect. The excavations at Saint-Rémy have revealed that the town of Glanum was captured by the Gauls during the second half of the 2nd century B.C. and that this was followed by some ten years of barbarian occupation immediately before the Roman conquest. The Gallo-Greek stelae of Glanum and the remains of structures with niches for human skulls bear witness to this sudden irruption of the Gauls into a hellenised city.

Thus in this last phase of town building and of Hellenistic influence we observe two quite distinct and separate worlds living side by side in southern Gaul, each going its own way, in a mutual relationship which was sometimes one of amity and sometimes one of hostility. On the one hand there were the colonies and trading stations on the coast, the hellenised towns of the interior and the Celt-iberian kingdoms of Languedoc, well disposed to their Greek neighbours; on the other the Celto-Ligurian tribes on the left bank of the Rhône and the Gallic tribes on the right bank. However much these tribes may have been exposed to influences from outside—which undoubtedly had a far-reaching effect on many aspects of their culture—they remained closer to their Celtic kinsmen in the north than to the citizens of Massilia, Agathe or Glanum.

Greek Traders and Italian Businessmen

In seeking to understand by what means Roman imperialism was able to get the better of the economic and cultural dynamism of the Greeks in the late 3rd and early 2nd century B.C. we can look to underwater archaeology for assistance. Thanks to underwater excavation, particularly at the Grand Congloué, we can observe the process by which Italian businessmen gained control of trade in the

Mediterranean. The cargo of the Grand Congloué wreck is dated by Benoit between 150 and 130 B.C. The voyage had been a joint Greek-Italian venture, the original Greek enterprise having been taken over by a group of Italian businessmen. The nature of the cargo indicates that the ship had sailed from Delos and headed, by way of Sicily and Campania, for its destination at Marseilles. This was in fact a later variant of the route originally charted by Massiliote seamen about 600 B.C.; but by now Italian businessmen were steadily becoming predominant in this trade, partly because of the increasing importance of the products of southern Italy (wine and Campanian pottery), partly because of the personalities of the men themselves.

Who were these businessmen? We know some of their names from inscriptions on amphoras or the stamps on the gypsum stoppers or caps with which they were sealed. The names on the stoppers probably belong to the owners of the vineyards which produced the wine; the names on the amphoras themselves were probably those of the merchants who exported it. The name Sestius, the one most commonly found on the amphora stamps of the Grand Congloué wreck, has been identified as that of a certain Marcus Sestius who is known to have lived on Delos in the early 2nd century B.C. This Marcus Sestius was granted Roman citizenship, along with a rich and generous Syracusan by the name of Timon, on the motion of Telemnestos, a Greek who had been responsible for restoring friendly relations between Delos and Rome about the year 192.

A certain Decimus Aufidius is associated with Sestius on the amphora stamps of the Grand Congloué. The Aufidii, who, like the Sestii, had probably come from Fregellae in Volscian territory, are known as merchants at Delos, Ostia and Puteoli at the beginning of the 2nd century B.C. Other names found on the stamps are those of the Juventii, an old family from Picenum with trading establishments at Salernum and Tarracina.

Thus, thanks to the material recovered by underwater archaeology, the study of pottery and epigraphy combine to give us a fuller and more personal understanding of the process by which the trade originally controlled by the Greeks was taken over first by Greek-Italian businessmen and later by Roman merchants. The successive changes in the shape of the amphoras themselves afford the clearest and most convincing evidence of this development. About 150 B.C. we can observe the switch from the Greek type of amphora, the commonest model at this period being the Rhodian, to the Roman type, by way of a transitional form which Benoit calls Greco-Italic. The large scale on which this transitional type was used was one of the revelations of the Grand Congloué excavations. The Roman type is less graceful than its predecessors but is sturdier and more functional, better adapted to methods of stowage designed to make the most economical use of the space in the ship's hold.

These first fruits of underwater archaeology throw a flood of light on a flourishing period of Mediterranean trade between 150 and 50 B.C. The beginning of this period coincides exactly with the Roman Republic's first ventures into Gaul, in both the economic and the diplomatic field.

Underwater exploration has also yielded much valuable information about the construction of ancient ships, and has cleared up a number of difficulties in Greek nautical terminology and in the written sources. Thus the passage in Homer comparing a row of axes with holes in them to the keel structure of a ship is explained by the discovery at the Grand Congloué of a keel bottom with the holes in the floor timbers running in a continuous line: and the examination of pieces of timber from the keel of the Grand Congloué wreck shows the survival into the Hellenistic period of Mediterranean techniques for the construction of the framework and planking which go back to the Egyptian Early and Middle Kingdom and are mentioned in Homer. A comparison of these timbers with a fragment of a 3rd century river barge found at Wantzenau, near Strasbourg, shows the radical difference between these archaic and traditionalist Mediterranean techniques and those adopted in northern Europe, using the more "modern" technique of steam bending in the fabrication of the frame.

The Origins of Gallic Religion

Most of our information about Gallic religion comes from Gallo-Roman monuments; but excavation is constantly bringing to light new pieces of evidence which enlarge our knowledge in this field.

The Gallic religious art of southern France, and in particular the important material found at Roquepertuse and Entremont, the iconography of which still remains extremely obscure, has been interpreted by Benoit as the expression of a purely Mediterranean community of ideas. This interesting theory, which rightly stresses the southern, and more specifically Greek, origin of certain Gallic religious practices and ritual structures, particularly the sanctuaries associated with springs, seems to me to err on the side of excessive generalisation. It takes no account of the distinctive individuality of Gallic religious conceptions, which is demonstrated not only in the Celto-Ligurian *oppida* of the 3rd to the 1st century B.C. but in the rest of Celtic territory—though the rest of the area has so far yielded little in the way of religious sculpture. Celto-Ligurian religious art cannot, in my view, be dissociated from the art which flourished in the Rhine and Moselle valleys in the 6th century B.C. The features peculiar to the Celts—historiated pillars, trunk figures, squatting figures, janus heads—seem to be represented everywhere in Gaul.

With this sculpture must be associated also the ornamental art and the decoration on pottery, which reflect the religious ideas and rituals characteristic of the continental Celts from the Hallstatt period to the end of La Tène.

Comparisons between the carving on the pillars and lintels of Mouriès, the repoussé ornament of bronze belts from southern Germany, Austria and eastern France, the decoration of certain Hallstatt situlas from northern Italy, Austria and Illyria, and the incised or moulded decoration of the Hallstatt vases of Austria, Bavaria and Hungary reveal a number of ritual and religious themes of frequent occurrence and great expressive force. Figures of men or women on horseback in association with representations of the sun are found at Mouriès and Le Pègue on pseudo-Ionian pottery and at Hagenau in the repoussé decoration of bronze belts *(Plate 19)*; stag-hunts and ritual sacrifices of stags are similarly found at Mouriès, in the incised decoration of pottery from Bavaria, Styria and Hungary, on a situla from Sesto Calende and in the rock carvings of the Val Camonica. Another figure which clearly played an important part was a kind of mother goddess, who was sometimes represented by herself, sometimes associated with a male divinity, and sometimes with two female attendants. On the votive waggon from Strettweg (Carinthia) this goddess is shown naked, bearing a kind of libation cup on her head and dwarfing with her superior height a group of naked warriors, both on foot and horseback, leading stags and rams.

A vase from Sopron in Hungary is decorated with incised ornament showing in an upper register two mother goddesses, one on either side of a single-handed encounter between two warriors bearing shields, with a stag-hunting scene in the lower register. Another vase with incised ornament from Sopron shows on one side three figures of mother goddesses raising their hands towards heaven, while a standing figure, attended by two horsemen, one of whom has dismounted and is standing in front of him, pours liquid from a bottle into another vessel; the dismounted rider is approaching a kind of altar, holding a bird in his right hand. The birds, the horsemen and the third figure are also found in association on a situla from Sesto Calende depicting the sacrifice of a stag.

We have also a number of bronze or pottery jars which are either decorated with figures of bovids or are themselves modelled in the form of bovids; they appear to be vessels for use in connection with sacrificial rites or libations of blood.

It seems likely that these scenes depict on the one hand figures from some archaic pantheon (solar horsemen), and on the other various acts of religious significance forming part of a ritual which was still a living force in Gallic religion at the end of the La Tène period and the beginning of the Gallo-Roman period—sacrifices of stags or bulls, armed gatherings in honour of the mother goddess or goddesses, duels between young warriors, and so on.

For the La Tène period the excavations in Champagne have made a valuable contribution to our knowledge. The funerary practices and the cult of the under-world gods, which go back to the Bronze Age, take on a new form in the cemeteries of the Marne area: square or rectangular funerary enclosures, heroes' tombs, votive pits, timber shrines dedicated to the cult of the dead and the divinities of the underworld. In recent excavations at Villeneuve-Renneville A. Brisson has discovered the remains of a domesticated stag wearing a bit which had been buried beside a Gallic warrior in a pit specially dug for the purpose: and we know that in the religion of the Gauls the sacrifice of a stag was a symbol of eternity. And we must undoubtedly interpret within the wider context of Gallic religious beliefs the sculptured figures from Roquepertuse and Entremont which still remain puzzling—the bird, the horses' heads, the paired janus heads and the squatting figures, sometimes with their hands resting on human heads. It may be that this last theme is related to the conflict between the sky god and the earth god, between Taranis and Esus.

The scenes represented in the relief decoration of certain votive cauldrons—the most important of which, the Brå, Rynkeby and Gundestrup cauldrons, are certainly of Gallic origin, although they were discovered in Denmark—seem to me less enigmatic and more expressive. On the Brå cauldron *(Plate 63)* there appears, between two bulls' heads, a curious expressionistic representation of an owl's head associated with a stylised snake. These seem to be the owl and snake of Athena, symbolising the Gallic mother goddess, associated with the bull sacrifice which took place every year in her honour. We also find a celticised Athena, probably representing the Celtic mother goddess, on the ornaments from Reinheim. On the Rynkeby cauldron is one of the oldest known forms of the Gallic divine triad—Esus in the form of a young man's head wearing a torc, Teutates in the shape of a boar and Taranis as a stylised wheel. And finally the rich iconography of the Gundestrup cauldron can be explained only by reference to works of Gallo-Roman art.

It thus appears that in the Hallstatt period there grew up in Celtic territory and in the Celto-Illyrian frontier areas a pantheon and religious ritual of Indo-European origin; and it is here that, in my view, we must look for the origins of Gallic religion. Much further study and excavation, however, will be necessary to fill out the picture which we can at present only dimly discern.

THE ROMANS IN GAUL

V

The Archaeological Evidence

There is little evidence dating from the Republican period in southern Gaul (Gallia Narbonensis). The recent discovery near Sigean of a milestone erected by Domitius Ahenobarbus *(Plate 70)*, victor over the Gauls and conqueror of the Province, has therefore been a particularly welcome contribution to our knowledge. It has enabled J. Campardou to establish more precisely on the ground the line of the oldest Roman road in Gaul; and P. M. Duval has set out, in a closely argued and persuasive study, the historical conclusions which can be drawn from this new piece of evidence and from comparison with the written sources on the early stages of the conquest and the colonisation of Gallia Narbonensis:

"The discovery of the milestone throws fresh light not only on the career of Domitius himself but also on the extension of Roman influence beyond the Alps and its civilising effect on southern Gaul... The romanisation of southern Gaul at once takes on enhanced significance." The conquest of the Province was not such an easy task as it appears in the accounts of certain historians. "We must now reconsider this judgment. The discoveries in the *oppida* reveal the high degree of civilisation attained by some of the native kingdoms." They also show that numerous fortified townships and hilltop refuge camps were established along the Mediterranean coast and in the Rhône valley at the end of the 2nd century and that this systematic occupation of hilltop sites continued until the time of Augustus.

Caesar's Siege Works

We have already noted in discussing the history of archaeology in France the important work done during the Second Empire in seeking out the traces left on the ground by Caesar's campaigns and battles in Gaul. These researches have been pursued by later scholars, sometimes on the same sites, as at Alise-Sainte-Reine, sometimes in quite new directions, for example in the Compiègne area (Matherat). Studies of this kind raise a variety of problems—the exact location of the events described by Caesar, whose accounts are not always as clear and exact as could be wished, and the technical details of his works of military engineering as they can be detected on the ground, with all that they can tell us about the tactics and methods of Roman military engineers at this period, the weapons and equipment of the opposing armies, and so on.

The discussion of questions of location has been, and will no doubt continue to be, bedevilled by endless arguments between local scholars, moved either by the patriotism of the parish pump or by the desire to make their names by producing a new and personal interpretation in a field where the main facts are well known but the exact geographical location and sequence of events may not be securely established.

Thus the site of the great final defeat of Vercingetorix has long been the subject of dispute between those who maintain that it was at Alaise in Franche-Comté and those who support the claims of Alise-Sainte-Reine; and the argument still goes on. This kind of rivalry may have useful results in so far as it provides a stimulus to serious study and fresh discoveries, but it may also lead to a fruitless squandering of effort in useless investigations and empty controversies. And if there is one site whose identification seems solidly established both by geographical, epigraphic and toponymical considerations and by archaeological excavation it is surely Alise. The discoveries made between 1861 and 1865 yielded convincing evidence that this was indeed the scene of the most dramatic, the bloodiest and the most decisive event in the war between Rome and Gaul. The most sceptical must surely be convinced by the result of these first excavations, which have been confirmed by the work done in our own day—the discovery in 1861 of the double ditches of contravallation and circumvallation (a La Tène sword, still in its scabbard, and a Hellenistic silver vase dating from a few years before the siege being found in the latter), the finding of bones of horses and warriors at the foot of Mont Rhéa, mingled with weapons, pieces of equipment and harness and many Gallic coins, and the clearance in 1864 of the great ditch, twenty feet across, which Caesar caused to be dug to protect his legionaries from a surprise attack while engaged on the siege works. These excavations have yielded precise and objective evidence on the works constructed by Caesar's troops (though the detailed structure and dimensions are not always exactly in line with the account given by Caesar himself—a circumstance which may perhaps be taken as an additional guarantee of authenticity) and enable us to re-live, two thousand years after the event, the most dramatic moments of the battle and the last desperate efforts of the Gallic defenders.

Matherat's more recent discoveries (1938–43) in the area round Clermont-de-l'Oise —at Breuil-le-Sec, Nointel and Catenoy—have revealed further examples of Caesar's military engineering, of a type not previously known from excavation and imperfectly understood, and have thrown fresh light on the methods of the Roman engineers. These are the brushwood bridges built by the legionaries at a critical stage in the campaign against the Bellovaci in order to advance rapidly across a marshy valley and take the enemy by surprise. Matherat's excavations in the peat bogs of Breuil-le-Sec enabled him to study the structure of two such bridges, with a roadway built up from sections prepared in advance resting on bundles of brushwood piled on top of one another in the water and kept in place by stakes driven into the river-bed. They also yielded important evidence in the form of pieces of dressed timber, stakes and other items used by the troops in the construction of trenches and other works, parts of a wheeled timber penthouse *(vinea)* and other material. These discoveries give us a completer and more exact understanding of the timber elements used in the construction of palisades and the reinforcement of ditches, and the Latin words take on a fuller and more concrete meaning.

The systematic investigation of a large Roman camp at Nointel and Catenoy, at the end of the hill of Liancourt, also enabled the excavator to define in much more precise detail the technique of construction of Caesar's trenches and to bring out the general principles on which they were based. The technique applied here was more complex, more varied and more subtle than at Alesia, and demonstrates the remarkable ingenuity of the Roman engineers. Another result of equal importance lay in the equivalences established between the actual evidence recovered by excavation and the Latin technical terms which had frequently been imperfectly understood and inadequately translated. Here again archaeology was able to enlarge our historical understanding.

Population Movements in the Early Stages of the Occupation

The early stages of the Roman occupation of Gaul raise a number of important problems which cannot be solved on the basis of the incomplete information we can glean from the written sources. Let us take one question as an example. Even though there was no longer any organised military resistance, does it follow that all opposition immediately came to an end throughout Gaul—which seems, administratively speaking, to have been controlled on a light rein and to have been occupied by relatively small forces at the end of the Republican period and in the early years of the Empire, when the bulk of the army was stationed on the frontiers?

This question can be answered only with the help of archaeology. The evidence to be considered is of three kinds:

1. The excavations of the *oppida*, of Gallic strongholds like Gergovia and Bibracte, have revealed a period of occupation and of town building which began between 40 and 30 B.C. and continued without a break until about 10 A.D.

The civilisation of this half century, during which Gaul was subjected to a relatively loose control by the Roman army and administration, seems to have been marked both by the rapid assimilation of certain Roman techniques (building, pottery) and by the maintenance of a social, economic and political structure dating from the period of independence. Thus it has been observed that at Gergovia the fortifications built during the final La Tène phase seem to have been restored, improved and altered at certain points. Apart from a few primitive huts near the walls, which contained nothing but Gallic pottery, much of it with roulette ornament, most of the buildings date from the same period: the dwelling houses, the craftsmen's workshops, the large *villae* and the sanctuary square are all of Augustan date. This does not mean that the *oppidum* was not occupied or used in the Gallic period: in fact it then served as a refuge and a gathering place, used particularly at times of danger or on the occasion of great religious festivals or regional fairs. The beginnings of permanent occupation and the earliest form of urban settlement can be dated to 40–30 B.C., when we may perhaps suppose that the Gauls were putting up a kind of passive resistance to the Roman administration by settling in the old strongholds of the Gallic war.

This period, which may be called Early Gallo-Roman, has a double interest. It demonstrates the survival of Gallic society and culture after the Roman conquest, and also bears witness to the rapidity with which the Gauls adopted and assimilated certain Roman techniques.

2. When we consider an *oppidum* in Bohemia like the Hradiště of Stradonice—well beyond the bounds of Gaul—we are astonished by the abundance of Gallic objects found there and the extraordinary resemblances in culture between this Bohemian settlement and the cities of central Gaul like Bibracte and Gergovia. The pottery and bronze articles of domestic use all belong to the Gallic culture of the final La Tène phase as it is found in Gaul proper, but the types of fibulas show that this culture belongs to the period after the Roman conquest and can be assigned to the beginnings of the Early Gallo-Roman phase. How are we to account for this? The explanation is given by a passage in Velleius Paterculus (II, 108–9) which relates how the Marcomanni, after their defeat by Drusus in 9 B.C., sought refuge in Bohemia. Here their leader, Marbod, founded a kingdom

76→

78, 79

84, 85

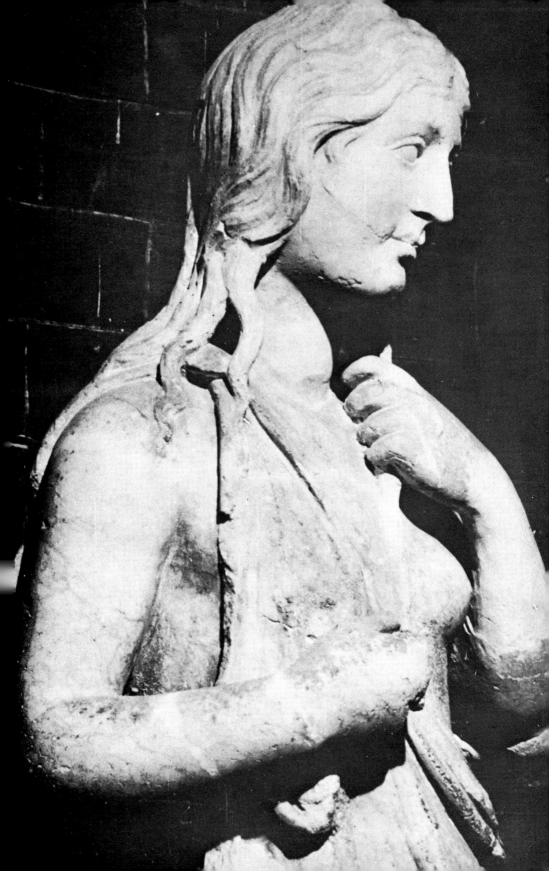

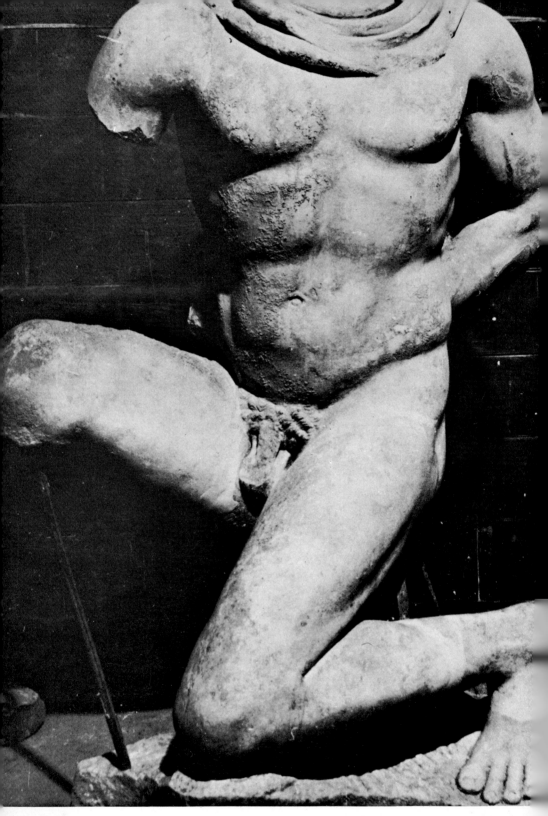

103

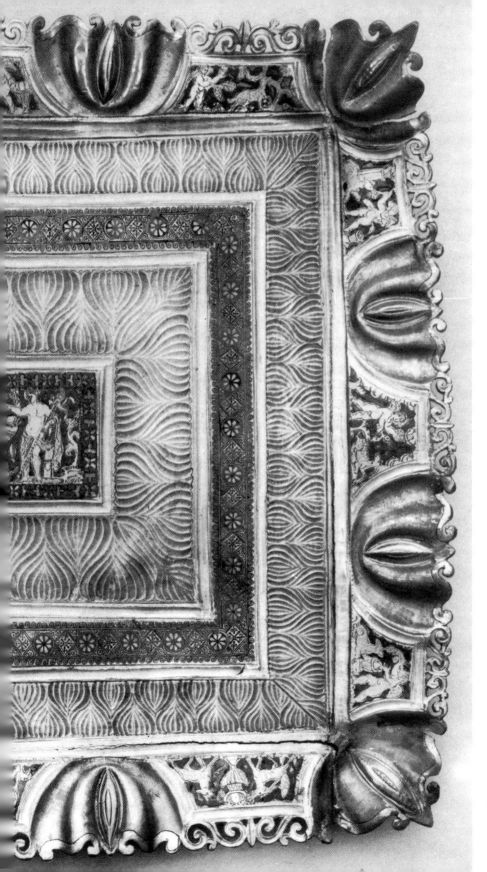

104

which provided a rallying place for tribes and individuals who sought to escape Roman control. Clearly the reference is to a party of Gauls who fled into exile before the advancing Romans and sought refuge among the Germans, in the new state established by Marbod and in what must have been the capital of that state on the Hradiště of Stradonice.

Evidence for this is provided by the material found on the Hradiště, consisting of Gallic pottery similar to that produced in Gaul itself and "provincial military" fibulas of Gallic or Norico-Pannonian type. This suggests that the *oppidum* was in effect colonised by emigrants from Gaul, Noricum and Pannonia; and we may recall that the Norico-Pannonian rebellion broke out in 6 A.D.

The reference in Velleius Paterculus is confirmed by a passage in Tacitus. Marbod's kingdom did not last long, for in 19 A.D. a Gothic noble named Catualda, who had previously been banished by Marbod, made his way into the territory of the Marcomanni, won over most of their leaders and captured Marbod's capital and his castle (Tacitus, *Annals*, II, 62). Here he found great quantities of booty which had been stored there by the Suevi, as well as numbers of victuallers and traders from the provinces captured by Rome, drawn to this distant foreign capital by the freedom of trade and the opportunities for profit which it offered. This emigration of Gauls into German territory is a historical fact which is vividly confirmed by the existence in Bohemia of a purely Gallic La Tène culture dating from the end of the 1st century B.C.

3. The high proportion of Gallic objects of La Tène III in the German cemeteries of the same period is undoubtedly connected with circumstances of a similar kind. It has been observed in particular that German tombs dating from the end of the 1st century B.C. and the beginning of the 1st century A.D. contain most of the Nauheim fibulas so far known. Indeed this observation led some scholars to draw erroneous conclusions about the northern origin and late date of this form of fibula, a typical product of La Tène III. In fact, as has been shown by recent discoveries in Provence and by excavations at Sainte-Blandine, near Vienne, the Nauheim fibula appeared in southern Gaul about 120 B.C. and had spread throughout the whole of Gaul before the Roman conquest. If none were found in the trenches at Alesia, this is because it was worn only by women. Later it was carried into Germany by Gauls fleeing from Roman control. It was because of these historical circumstances that the culture of the southern and western Germans took on such a strong Gallic tinge at this period. The fibulas are not the only Gallic objects

found in the tombs: the weapons, the ornaments, the pottery and the whole of the material culture of the Germans living on the borders of Gaul were deeply imbued with Gallic influences. The refugees fleeing before the Roman conquest did in fact establish cultural and economic contacts which were to persist throughout the Roman period.

Panorama of Roman Gaul

The application of stratigraphic methods, formerly applied mainly to prehistoric sites, has made it possible to establish the history of large Gallo-Roman cities like Strasbourg and Metz or small centres of craft production like Seltz and Ehl and to define their periods of destruction and reconstruction. Comparisons between a number of sites which have been studied in this way will then allow us to trace some of the major historical factors which conditioned the development of culture in north-eastern Gaul; for it was political and military events, and particularly the various crises caused by mutinies and invasions, which provided the framework for this development. This is demonstrated in the most concrete way by the evidence obtained from stratigraphic excavations; and such excavations also throw light on certain geographical or climatic factors, disregarded or imperfectly understood, which undoubtedly influenced the material conditions of human life. Let us attempt to sketch out the historical picture which emerges from the stratigraphic evidence so far available.

The Historical Stratigraphy of North-Eastern Gaul

It is important to note, in the first place, that in many cases the earliest structures, dating from the Augustan period, whatever their original character (e.g., hut bases or remains of timber buildings), stood close to a cobbled street or road built on top of the natural ground level. This demonstrates at once the first concern of the Roman authorities—to promote communications and the transport of goods by the provision of metalled roads.

The first destruction level, separating these remains from later ones, is that of 21 A.D., which has been observed at Metz, Ehl and Sarrebourg. It seems to have been followed at Metz by a horizon containing buildings which are already romanised, with terrazzo floors and frescoed walls. This first period of Roman-style buildings, a period of considerable architectural achievement, was interrupted by the destructions of 68–70 A.D. for which there is evidence throughout the whole of the area covered by our investigations, from Daspich-Ebange near Thionville to Biesheim-Künheim near Colmar by way of Metz, Sarrebourg, the Col de Saverne, Strasbourg, Seltz, Ehl and other cities.

In the Rhine valley, particularly at Ehl and Biesheim-Künheim, we find beds of natural gravel, pointing to heavy flooding by the river, between the remains of the earliest structures and the conflagration level of 70 A.D. Other evidence at Strasbourg *(Plates 2–4)* (Rue de l'Ail, Ruelle St Médard) shows that there was a general rise in the water table, accompanied by frequent floods, after 50 A.D. Is this to be attributed to a period of heavy rainfall or to subsidence of the normal ground surface in the Rhine depression? The fact that Dr Planson made similar observations at Les Bolards in Burgundy, in an excavation carried out with the most rigorous method, suggests that the former explanation is more likely to be correct. This period of frequent spates, with serious flooding at intervals, seem to have lasted in the Rhine valley from 60 A.D. to the end of the 2nd century.

In almost every case—at Strasbourg, Metz, Sarrebourg, the Col de Saverne, Ehl and Seltz—a conflagration level dating from the end of the 1st century overlies the destruction of the year 70. These various observations, taken together, prove that in the reign of Nerva eastern Gaul was ravaged by the consequences of a military mutiny which broke out in the Rhineland and the Agri Decumates. More recently evidence of a similar kind has been observed at Heidelberg by Heukemes. Examination of the 2nd century levels yields evidence of a long period of tranquillity lasting from Trajan to Marcus Aurelius, marked by large-scale road construction accompanied by the building up and consolidation of the ground surface. At various points in Strasbourg traces have been observed of two destructions at the end of the 2nd century, probably the result of incursions by Germanic tribes or military rebellions in the reign of Marcus Aurelius or Commodus, at some time between 170 and 180.

The remains of Severan buildings and floor levels are overlaid by a substantial destruction and conflagration level, now reliably dated to the year 235, at the end of the reign of Alexander Severus. Was this connected with an invasion by the Alamanni, or with fighting between different legions following the rebellion by the army based on Mainz and the murder of Alexander Severus and his mother Julia Mammaea? Whatever the nature of these events, they left spectacular evidence of armed conflict and savage and systematic destruction—the remains of a battlefield at Koenigshoffen and a variety of weapons, implements, equipment and ballista missiles abandoned in the charred ruins of military hutments under the church of St Etienne in Strasbourg.

These events marked the beginning of a period of military anarchy. At Strasbourg the camp was rebuilt by the successors of the Severi, and the fortress, after being reoccupied and reinstated by the Eighth Legion, became a strong point in the defence system of the Rhineland and was thus preserved from capture and destruction. At Metz and Saverne, on the other hand, further destruction and conflagration levels dated to the 3rd century bear witness to the havoc wrought in the open towns by the invaders. We find the same thing happening at *vici* like Ehl, Seltz or Sarre-Union and *villae* like those at St Ulrich or Mackwiller. It is clear that the bands of marauding Alamanni and Franks avoided the well defended legionary fortresses and turned against the settlements which offered no organised resistance (end of 3rd and beginning of 4th century).

On all the Roman sites the Tetrarchy and the reign of Constantine were periods of reconstruction during which the pattern of both urban and rural life was fundamentally transformed. This seems to be the case not only with cities like Metz or Strasbourg, which altered their street layout, but with the *vici* and *villae*, and indeed the sanctuaries as well. In some of the sanctuaries, as at Mackwiller, there is frequently a return to indigenous traditions.

The period of rebuilding and intense activity in the first half of the 4th century was brutally interrupted by the catastrophe of 352. Recent excavations have established the date of this (coin hoards of Mackwiller, Strasbourg, St Etienne and Villing) and revealed its extent. They have also demonstrated with great clarity that the urban and rural communities suffered a fearful blow from which they were slow to recover: even where life returned to the sites, often after a long interruption, it was a poverty-stricken existence in wretched dwellings patched up amid the ruins.

The impressive building and rebuilding effort of the reigns of Valentinian and Gratian extended only to the cities and to certain favoured regions like the Trier area and the Moselle valley. In most places life was precarious and insecure, and a general stagnation set in. We have very tangible proof of this in the makeshift structures put together from the debris of demolished buildings which have been brought to light in the excavations on the Ruelle St Médard site in Strasbourg. The end of the 4th and the beginning of the 5th century were marked by two further destructions, but few traces of these have survived at either Metz or Strasbourg, since the levels corresponding to these events are fairly high in the stratigraphic sequence and have for the most part been destroyed by the construction of cellars in later periods. The fires started by the Huns in 451, however, are clearly attested at Strasbourg (church of St Etienne) *(Plates 1, 5)*.

One of the most interesting points about the Ruelle St Médard excavations in Strasbourg was their demonstration that a Gallo-Roman community had settled round a Christian church in a corner of the ruined *castrum* (church of St Etienne) in the 5th century, leading a hazardous and precarious existence while the barbarians were establishing themselves in the surrounding countryside and on the outskirts of the town. The cemeteries used by this community have been found. Similar observations have been made in Switzerland, at Augst, Windisch and Basle. It seems, therefore, that the new arrivals did not settle in the towns, now more than half destroyed, but took up their abode in the countryside round them. The incomers in this region were Alamanni: in the Cologne area the Franks occupied the same cemeteries and used the same churches as the Gallo-Romans. The research which has made it possible to give this historical account of happenings in eastern Gaul has increased our knowledge in two main respects. In the first place, it has shown the dire effects which these events had on the life of the people of the area. Secondly, it has given us a clear and objective picture of developments over the centuries and has enabled us to put exact dates on the different stages. The sequence of events can be summarised as follows:

30 B.C. to 21 A.D.: Early Gallo-Roman period; the crisis of 21.

21–70 A.D.: period of romanisation, from Tiberius to Nero; the crisis of 68–70.

70–97 A.D.: Flavian period; the crisis of 97.

97–190 A.D.: period of peace and prosperity; crisis between 170 and 180.

190–235 A.D.: Severian period; the crisis of 235.

235–284 A.D.: period of anarchy; crises of 244, 260 and 270; the great invasions of 275–277.

284–352 A.D.: first restoration of the Late Empire; the invasions of 352–355.

355–383 A.D.: second restoration of the Late Empire.

383–455 A.D.: period of anarchy and invasions (383, 407–408, 451); the end of Roman Gaul.

The Development of Gallic Provincial Civilisation

The period during which Gallic traditions survived (and which we have called Early Gallo-Roman) seems to have lasted, with variations from area to area, throughout the reign of Augustus and into that of Tiberius, until it was cut short about the year 21 A.D. The Claudian period which followed was an age of prosperity and reorganisation during which romanisation made rapid strides. At the end of the 1st century, with its successive crises in 68–70 and 97, there seem to have been resurgences of national feeling among the Gauls. Thereafter, however, the Flavian period, with its military recovery, its redistribution of land and its measures to revive the economy, enabled Rome to regain full control of the province. The period of peace and civil harmony inaugurated by Trajan and his successors promoted the economic life and social development of Gaul and encouraged the flowering of its culture in many directions. This also led to the emergence of marked provincial differences, as a result of the new contacts which were now established between different parts of the Empire, using channels of communication—and this is a significant development—which no longer always passed through Rome. At the end of the 2nd century a variety of causes, both economic and social (the rural exodus and the settlement of native Gauls in the towns, combined with Oriental influences) led to some revival of national feeling in art and religion and also to a curious interaction between different national cultures, including elements contributed by the countryfolk of Gaul and the peoples of the East. From this mingling of cultures there emerged a kind of syncretism which was expressed in the various aspects of material culture, art and religion. The Severan period saw a continuance of this trend, but at the same time, as a result of the new threats looming up on the frontiers of Germany, brought a certain reaction in the western provinces which was to bear fruit at a later stage, towards the end of the 3rd century.

The long period of crises which began in 235 led the Gauls to reflect on their situation and to assess the value of what Rome and Roman civilisation had done for them. There was a vigorous revival of the old Gallic traditions, accompanied by the emergence of a spontaneous desire among the Gauls to defend with their own national strength a common inheritance which Rome—torn by military rebellion and racked by political rivalries—was no longer able to preserve. What emerges —however dimly—from the work so far done by excavators and scholars on this troubled period during the 3rd century is an impression of chaos and a descent into barbarism, no doubt, but also of a new and spontaneously created form of *romanitas*, a popular culture in which Gallic traditions play their part in close association with those features of Roman civilisation which had been preserved by the people of Gaul and incorporated into the substance of their life. The beginning of the 4th century was marked by an intense programme of reconstruction which profoundly modified all existing structures; but while this was going on in the towns the country areas were returning to the older traditions of Gaul. This process was helped by the fact that the German *foederati* (members of tribes allied with Rome) and the *laeti* (barbarian mercenaries) who were now settled in these areas brought with them a pattern of customs and techniques and a way of life which went back to prehistoric times. This culture of the *laeti*, developing alongside the resurgences of Gallic culture and the renewal of Roman civilisation, is the first foreshadowing of Merovingian culture.

The catastrophe of 352 marked a new setback, and for most of the population meant the beginning of a period of uncertainty and danger which continued through the dark centuries of the invasions and the early Middle Ages. In certain areas, however—particularly round Trier and in the Moselle valley or in southwestern Gaul—the second restoration of the Empire provided a setting for the brilliant and eclectic culture of a highly romanised aristocracy. After the great invasion of 407—the first stage in the spread of Germanic influence—the major fact is the existence of two worlds living side by side: the Christian Gallo-Roman communities concentrated in the towns and on the great estates, the Germanic tribes settling in the country and taking over the land for their own use.

The main points which emerge from this rapid survey of the development of civilisation in Gaul can be summarised very briefly. The pattern of social and cultural transformations shows a regular alternation between periods of intensive romanisation and periods in which there was a revival of native feeling, with the latter trend prevailing from the end of the 2nd century onwards. It was these vicissitudes which forged the distinctive personality of the province and contributed to its complexity.

The factors which made possible the romanisation of Gaul were the Roman army, with its social and civilising rôle; the development of the rural areas, involving a new pattern of land ownership and the provision of the necessary equipment and services; the spread of technical improvements and the development of industry; the growth of trade; and the Roman Imperial cult and politico-religious propaganda.

The preservation of the distinctive personality of the Gauls and the survival of native tradition can be attributed to the existence of areas of native conservatism outside the romanised areas; the movement of the native population from the rural areas into the towns from the 2nd century onwards; the political crises and periodic revivals of native feeling (end of 1st century, 3rd century) and the mechanisms of inter-provincial trade, with the introduction of Oriental influences, which brought out certain tendencies latent in the native population of the towns.

The distinctive personality of the province was expressed in its particular farming methods; in certain types of buildings and urban structures; in its special industries and techniques; in the local schools of popular art and to a certain extent also in the main regional schools; and in funerary rites, customs and beliefs and religious forms and practices.

The First Romanising Forces

The presence in Germany, on the Rhine and along the *Limes,* of a large army whose strength ranged according to circumstances between fifty thousand and a hundred thousand men and which was for long the most considerable force in the Empire, had a variety of consequences going far beyond the military sphere. It was the army which gave the provinces of eastern and northern Gaul their distinctive political character. It was round the army, and on the basis of the army's needs, that there was established a large economic region taking in the Rhineland, the glacis area of the Agri Decumates and the hinterland of the neighbouring cities in northern and eastern Gaul. It was to permit the rapid movement of reinforcements that a network of roads was constructed linking the Rhine valley directly with the Danube and northern Italy. The Roman army itself carried on a wide range of activities, but it also gave an impetus to innumerable other activities, not only in its immediate area of operation but throughout the whole province. It was both a centre of attraction and a focus of influences radiating in many directions, and was undoubtedly one of the most active and effective factors in the process of romanisation.

The Civilising Influence of the Legions

In the Roman cities of the Rhineland and the camps on the *Limes* the soil has yielded up large quantities of weapons and equipment, remains of fortified camps and barrack blocks, inscriptions and figured monuments. Military archaeology has now become a specialty which is making an increasingly important contribution to our knowledge of Roman history. It operates rather like an espionage service concerned to ferret out the military secrets of ancient times. Its first object is to collect all the available evidence which will enable it to establish the movements of bodies of troops—legions, auxiliary cohorts, *alae* and *numeri* of cavalry—at different times; and in this quest it supplements the information recorded by the historians and such administrative documents as the *Notitia Dignitatum* with the evidence which can be gleaned from inscriptions on stone, legionary stamps on tiles, funerary monuments, weapons and other objects, as well as from the remains of military camps and hutments.

The interest and importance of this information on the history of the legions and the auxiliary corps goes far beyond the purely military field. In particular it provides exact points of reference, chronological signposts which are valid for areas outside the military zone. Thus by detailed examination of the bas-reliefs on the triumphal arch at Orange *(Plates 132–134)* and comparison with military stelae from the Rhineland it has been possible to establish the exact date and purpose of this important monument. Whereas it had long been thought, on the basis of superficial examination, that the Orange bas-reliefs dated from the time of Caesar and depicted scenes from the Gallic war, an analysis of the weapons and equipment shown in the main friezes has proved that the fighting was between the cavalry of the Second Legion (whose shields bore the emblem of the legion, a capricorn) and German mercenaries and rebellious Gauls. These engagements took place in 21 A.D., during the reign of Tiberius, in the Metz-Trier area, when the legion was on garrison duty at Strasbourg. Orange was a colony of veterans of the Second Legion, and the arch commemorates a second settlement of colonists in the reign of Tiberius, with allusions to the battles in which the soldiers of the legion had so recently distinguished themselves. And thus we now have an exact date for one of the finest known ensembles of provincial sculpture in Gaul.

The important consequences which often followed movements of legions from one province to another have long been recognised. The transfer of troops from the Danube to the Rhine after the campaign of the year 70 had the effect of bringing eastern Gaul into much more direct contact with the Balkans and the hellenised Orient. For example the Eighth Legion, coming from Moesia, on the lower Danube, introduced certain Oriental influences during the period of the Flavians. Recent excavations have shown that Greek was written at Strasbourg at the end of the

1st century, and religious as well as artistic influences made themselves felt on a considerable scale. Strasbourg, a small township of no particular importance at the end of Nero's reign, became in the middle of the 2nd century the point of entry of religious influences (the cult of Mithra) as well as artistic influences coming from the East by way of the Danube valley. Between the reigns of Antoninus and Septimius Severus the Strasbourg schools of sculpture rose to considerable importance and seem to have had an extensive sphere of influence in the Rhineland and the neighbouring cities.

Excavations of camps in Germany, ranging in date from Augustus to the Flavians (Haltern, Oberaden, Neuss, Xanten), and of the *Limes* have yielded a rich harvest of information about the work of the Roman forces and their conditions of life. Thus we can observe in the early Empire the development of a regular system of what might be called military town planning, starting with temporary camps like the one at Oberaden and culminating in the construction of permanent settlements notable for their functional character and logical clarity of layout. There is a very striking difference between the earliest camps (Haltern, Oberaden) and the latest (Xanten, Neuss). Two main trends can be observed. On the one hand there is a steady increase in the space occupied by the increasingly sumptuous residences of the officers (e.g., the legates' palace at Xanten), by administrative buildings (the *praetorium* and its associated buildings) and by medical services (the *valetudinarium*). On the other hand, particularly from the 2nd century onwards (cf. the camps on the *Limes*), there is an improved standard of amenities for the troops, leading to the provision of baths inside the camps or in the immediate neighbourhood. In the structure of the fortifications themselves we can observe such changes, from the time of Hadrian onwards, as the establishment of fixed defensive lines and the construction of stone towers and *castella* in place of earlier timber structures.

Apart from these purely military installations, mention must also be made of the *canabae*, the associated settlements of booths and workshops set up by craftsmen and traders in the immediate vicinity of the camps. Some of these—as at Mainz, Bonn, Xanten, Cologne and Strasbourg—are of considerable size, amounting to small towns in their own right. It was the *canabarii* of Mainz who presented to Nero in 66 A.D. a monumental column decorated with carving which is one of the masterpieces of provincial sculpture.

The legion was an important centre of economic activity, with its own stores and supply depots and its own workshops. At Strasbourg the Eighth Legion established its own potters' workshop and its own tile-making shop, first near the River Ill on the line of the present-day Rue de l'Ail and later at the western end of the *vicus* of Koenigshoffen, on the Saverne road. The excavations in the Rue de l'Ail have shown that in the time of the Flavians the legionary potters manufactured large quantities of pottery vessels, lamps and other articles for the use of the army. Other workshops of the same type have been found at Windisch (Vindonissa) in Switzerland and at Holdeurn in Holland.

The rubbish pits and waste heaps attached to the legionary camps may on occasion yield interesting material. Thus an important find was made in a large rubbish pit on a hillside above a river near Windisch, in the form of a number of fragments of leather. The study of these fragments produced much new information and made it possible to date the first appearance in the Roman soldier's uniform of the leather tunics, breeches, breastplate sections and shoulderpieces which were unknown in the early days of the Empire but seem to have been in regular use by the time of the carvings on Trajan's Column. It appears probable that the practice of wearing this leather equipment was brought in under the Flavians by troops from the Danube area and Rhaetia, who had no doubt acquired the habit from the native populations of those areas. The modern observer cannot help being reminded of the *Lederhosen* worn by the peasants of Bavaria.

The Redistribution of Land

In discussing the various means by which Roman civilisation penetrated into Gaul there is frequently a tendency to concentrate too exclusively on urban life and the process of urbanisation. In fact, however, the romanisation of the rural areas went ahead *pari passu* with that of the towns, its instruments being the introduction of the Roman cadastral registers, the extension to the province of the types of estate and farm holdings found elsewhere in the Empire, and the considerable effort devoted by the Romans to the organisation of agriculture and the provision of the necessary equipment and services.

One of the most durable and most spectacular proofs of the extent of Roman influence on the outlying provinces is provided by the remains of ancient landholding patterns. The extensive colonial centuriation of Tunisia were revealed by air photography some ten years ago; and for Gaul we now possess the remarkable cadastral records of Orange, the remains of plans and registers engraved on marble which in ancient times were displayed in a public building in the town. These were first brought to light by a casual find during earth-moving operations, and the missing pieces were then recovered by systematic excavation. They are one of the oldest land registers known, a unique discovery which is of the very greatest interest. With the help of air photography certain parts of the register have been matched with the remains of the ancient pattern of property boundaries which can still be detected on the ground.

Similar studies, based on air photography and the interpretation of maps, have been carried out more recently in Alsace by E. Juillard, G. Lévy-Mertz, J. Braun, A. Stieber and the present author. They have revealed ancient cadastral systems along the line of Roman roads in Lower Alsace, in the Erstein, Sélestat and Saverne areas. Two types of pattern have been observed: one based on a complete *centuria*, with units 710 metres square, the other based on half a *centuria*, with units measuring 355 by 710 metres. The former type seems to date from the Flavian period and the colonisation of the Agri Decumates, since an exactly similar pattern can be found on the other bank of the Rhine, in the territory of Baden. The second type, the counterpart to which has been found in the Alzey area, may date from the Late Empire and the settlement of the *laeti* and *foederati*, in the reign of either Constantine or Valentinian. It is surely a fascinating thought that the field boundaries drawn by the Roman *agrimensores* more than two thousand years ago can still be detected, fragmentary no doubt but frequently showing a coherent pattern, in the country tracks and field boundaries of our own day.

Cadastral records like those of Orange served a variety of purposes: they were the basis of the farming structure of the area, they constituted a title to property, and they were official records of ownership for the purposes of tax assessment. The great uniform registers prepared under government authority in colonial territories and recently acquired areas still under military rule had their counterparts in the similar registers of private property in the areas under civil administration: the official registers served in effect as models and examples for the free landowners seeking to organise their properties on a rational basis.

The Transformation of Rural Life

Archaeology has shown that the salient fact in the development of the rural areas of Gaul was the generalisation of the Roman system of the *fundus* and the *villa*. Innumerable remains of *villae* or Roman farms have been found scattered about the countryside of France—sometimes structures of considerable size, usually on sites different from those of the present-day villages. Some excellent studies have been published in this field by such scholars as the late Albert Grenier. The problems involved are of great economic and social importance.

The Gauls did not practise the Roman system of working the *fundus* as we know it from the Roman agricultural writers—i.e., as a closed economy. The *fundus* was required to be self-sufficient and to make a profit for the owner by the sale of surplus produce; and accordingly the pattern of farming covered a very wide range, including cereals, fruit and vegetables, livestock, timber and of course the one dominant crop of the Mediterranean area, the vine. The *fundus* was a property of some size belonging to a fairly well-to-do landowner, who was able to rely on an abundant supply of manpower—mainly slave labour—to work his land.

The Gallic system, in so far as we can establish it, was based on small-scale land ownership. The farmers of Gaul were free men living in small communities in villages or hamlets and exchanging their produce in local markets, which seem to have played a central part in the economy. These markets, often held in the *oppida*, were apparently controlled by a kind of feudal lord or knight, the peasants and craftsmen being in some sense his vassals.

The expansion of the *fundus* and the *villa* at the expense of the farming villages and hamlets of native type—which still, however, survived in the less fertile areas and those less suited to the varied farming pattern of the *fundus*—seems to have been conditioned mainly by the disappearance of the feudal lords of Gallic origin and the rise of new social classes enriched by trade and industry who were anxious to put their money into land. This trend was partly spontaneous, partly directed and encouraged by the Roman authorities, in particular by the army, which was creating new patterns of land use based on the cadastral registers and sometimes even establishing model farms for its veterans in colonies and newly annexed territories.

The *villa* of Mayen, which was excavated with exemplary competence by Oelmann, gives us the opportunity to study in detail the development and transformation of a native hut into a Roman *villa*, which was steadily enlarged throughout the 1st and 2nd centuries to make it increasingly more comfortable and more functional. We can thus observe the rise in the living standards of the smaller free landowners attached to the soil in the favourable conditions provided by the Roman peace. The *villa* of Müngersdorf, near Cologne, which was excavated and studied by F. Fremersdorf, illustrates the establishment of a model farm on a new site in colonial territory during the reign of Nero, comprising a comfortable and well planned house for the owner, living accommodation and refectories for the slave labour, and carefully designed and remarkably well equipped farm buildings —granaries, silos, hay-lofts, cattle stalls, stables, pigsties, a sheepfold, and so on. Here we can observe the ingenious efforts of the architects and agricultural specialists to apply the principles of Roman agriculture in rural Gaul, with the help of properly planned farm buildings.

The *villa* of Martres-Tolosane, excavated by L. Joulin, shows the development of a country mansion belonging to a family of large landowners and the organisation of the considerable property attached to it. This type of large estate, transplanted from Italy to Gaul, tended to develop mainly in the areas round the larger cities in which big business flourished, as in Aquitaine and the Moselle valley. It reflects the rise of a rich and highly romanised governing class which by the end of the Empire was well on the way to becoming a regular feudal class. These sumptuous mansions, decorated with rich mosaics, sculpture and marble, were the homes of an aristocratic caste, cultivated and extremely eclectic in their tastes, and enjoying a standard of life which in no way fell short of that of their counterparts in other Roman provinces.

In this expanding agricultural economy there is one type of site, undoubtedly based on native traditions, which takes on particular importance in Gaul. This is the township built round a sanctuary, of which examples have been found at Sanxay, Chassenon, Champlieu, Vieil-Evreux and elsewhere. These are not towns in the proper sense of the term, for there are hardly any houses. They do, however, have some of the public buildings found in a town—a basilica, baths, a theatre, an amphitheatre—usually situated round a sanctuary and a market. To a large extent these sites represent a survival of native traditions, but they also show a high degree of romanisation, demonstrating clearly that the building effort was not confined to the towns, and that the towns were not the only factors in the assimilation of Roman culture. These sites were meeting places used by the country people of the surrounding district for economic, cultural and religious purposes, where some of the amenities and products of the cities were made available to country dwellers.

What was the effect of the great invasions on this immense investment of capital resources in the rural areas, based as it was on a stable agrarian structure? The older theories which sought to identify the ancient pattern of land ownership in the countryside of our own day (Camille Jullian) are valid only in certain favoured areas. Some large estates have in fact survived all the vicissitudes of history and have been preserved in their entirety, as a result of particularly favourable circumstances—perhaps because they became royal property or fell into the ownership of an abbey, or because they were situated in an area which remained untouched by invasions. In most cases, however, the pattern of land ownership has been profoundly changed by the various disturbances which have taken place over the centuries, beginning in ancient times. In the 4th century the Emperors brought in Germanic settlers and redistributed the land in the devastated and depopulated rural areas. The pattern of distribution of the *villae* and great estates of the early Empire in the invasion areas often bears no relationship to the pattern of occupation in the late Empire. This later pattern may coincide in some cases with that found in prehistoric or protohistorical times: thus the sites of the Gallic cemeteries in Champagne seem to have been systematically reoccupied by *laeti* and *foederati* in the 4th century. The exhaustive studies now being carried out on the sites of Roman and protohistorical settlements, both by air photography and by planned excavation on the ground, have revealed the complexity of the problems involved and the variety of different local situations. The distribution of the *villae* in the Somme valley, recently mapped by Agache, shows no relationship to the present-day pattern of occupation.

107   108

112

113

114

117→

115   116

122

123

124

125

127

128

129

ASPECTS OF GALLO-ROMAN CIVILISATION

The Towns

We have noted in the previous chapter that the traditional theory of the predominance of the towns in Roman Gaul cannot be accepted without qualification. To say this, however, is not to minimise the decisive contribution made by the towns to the process of romanisation.

The origins of Gallo-Roman town building go back a long way, and it can no longer be maintained that the Romans were the first to establish towns in Gaul. As early as the end of the 6th century B.C. we see fortified and regularly planned cities being erected, like those of the Heuneburg, Le Pègue or Mont Lassois. At the end of the 4th century a Gallo-Greek town building movement was in progress, attested by the spectacular remains which have been brought to light at Ensérune, Saint-Blaise and Le Cayla de Mailhac, and this movement continued in the 3rd and 2nd centuries at Saint-Rémy.

Independent Gaul also had some kind of urban development before the arrival of the Romans, though this did not date so far back as the Gallo-Greek towns. The town of Avaricum is described by Caesar as having a forum, streets and squares. Evidence of this native town building has also been provided by the excavations at Bibracte and Gergovia: these towns were built and organised at a time when Roman influence had barely begun to make itself felt, and they were certainly based on native traditions. The forum of Bibracte gives us an example of a Gallic place of assembly—a "sanctuary square", with lines of booths round the sides, which owes nothing to Roman influence and is evidently a purely indigenous type of urban structure.

The process of romanisation, however, introduced new patterns of town building, and the native type of forum was now usually relegated to the regional sanctuaries. There seems nevertheless to have been a square of this kind in the Roman camp at Argentoratum, still occupying its original site and laid out on a different orientation from the camp.

Town Planning

In general, a provincial Roman town was laid out on a regular plan, with a rectangular grid based on two axes running at right angles to one another, the *cardo* and the *decumanus*. The orientation was fixed by taking a sighting on the sun on a particular day in the year, the day on which the town was founded: a practice which enabled A. Audin to use the orientation of the *decumanus* at Lyons as a pointer to the date of foundation of the city.

We must not suppose, however, that all the Roman towns in Gaul were built on the same uniform plan. The town layouts which have been recovered include numerous irregularities, resulting either from the nature of the terrain, the survival of features from some earlier period, or some other special factor. Indeed the principle of the rectangular grid does not seem to have become generally accepted until the conquest of the Three Gauls. Some towns in the south with a layout of Hellenistic origin like Glanum, or of Republican date like Vaison, show a regular plan which is neither square or rectangular but in the shape of a trapezium or a triangle—an arrangement commonly found in the Hellenistic towns of the West, as for instance on Delos.

Even within a plan which is basically rectangular, irregularities and distortions may result from the intrusion of oblique lines continuing the direction of main roads entering the town: this is the case, for example, at Autun, Nîmes and Lyons. Sometimes, too, as at Augst, the town may have been formed by the juxtaposition and amalgamation of two rectangular layouts on different orientations. In the town of the Rauraci one of the two plans is that of the Roman settlement, the other that of a group of sanctuaries of native origin. An association of the same kind is found at Strasbourg-Argentoratum.

Whatever the exact plan, however, the ancient city always had one distinctive feature—a central point and meeting place at the junction of the two main streets, the *cardo* and the *decumanus*. This focal point, the layout of which is much more regular in the provinces than at Rome itself or elsewhere in Italy, consists essentially of a forum, with which a "sanctuary square" *(capitolium)* is sometimes associated.

The town centre may take a number of different forms. In small towns in the military areas, particularly in Germany and Britain, its plan is frequently modelled on the *praetorium* of a Roman camp. Usually, however, it is laid out on a fairly simple plan—a long rectangular open space surrounded by porticoes and shops, a basilica, a *curia* and various administrative buildings. This is the type most commonly found in the smaller and middle-sized towns. The former type may be called the "military provincial" type, the latter the "civil provincial" type.

Some of the larger towns, containing a provincial or regional sanctuary of the Imperial cult, seem to have followed the model of the Imperial fora in Rome, adopting a plan which comprised a forum with an adjoining square occupied by a temple dedicated to Rome and Augustus. This type is found, for example, at Saint-Bertrand-de-Comminges, Narbonne, Arles, Nîmes and Paris; it might be labelled the "Augustan Imperial" type. At a later date Trajan's forum and markets had a considerable influence on the provincial towns, and were imitated even by small townships like Alesia; this type might be called the "2nd century Imperial" type.

Some Typical Buildings

Of these monumental town centres, the pride of their citizens, considerable remains have survived on numerous sites—e.g., the temples of Nîmes and Vienne and the cryptoporticuses of Narbonne, Reims, Arles and Bavay.

What was the function of the cryptoporticuses, those striking structures which have been identified in a number of large Gallo-Roman towns? Briefly, they are underground galleries excavated or constructed under the forum; they were not, however, exclusively associated with fora, for quite recently a cryptoporticus has been found associated with a procurator's palace at Trier dating from the 2nd century. They are often decorated with frescoes, suggesting that they were some kind of public promenade. It has also been suggested that they were used for storing reserve supplies of grain, oil and wine (Arles, Bavay, Reims).

Among the buildings associated with the forum the basilicas were of particular importance. These were large halls comprising one or more bays, sometimes with terminal or lateral apses. Often of considerable size, they were designed to hold large numbers of people, and were frequently the meeting place of municipal assemblies, lawcourts, etc. The development of the civil basilica is particularly interesting in the western part of the Empire, and especially in Gaul. It seems originally to have formed part of the complex of buildings which constituted the town centre, the main focus of municipal and judicial activity in the town. Then in the 2nd century, perhaps as a result of Hadrian's administrative reform, it became the central feature of the governor's palace or, as at Trier, the procurator's. At Trier the procuratorial basilica was succeeded in the reign of Constantine by a new basilica designed by the Emperor to serve as the *aula palatina (Plate 91)* or throne room. A double basilica built in the vicinity some time later is the prototype in the West of the great Christian cathedrals; it seems to have both served as court and parish church, and was renovated, extended and heightened in the reign of Gratian.

Other basilicas of smaller size, like those at Metz (Saint-Pierre-aux-Nonnains) and Strasbourg (Saint-Etienne), were built in the 4th or 5th century, within the ramparts but at some distance from the town centre. As they do not seem to be associated with a market or a procurator's palace it is possible that these were also Christian churches, although this cannot yet be definitely proved. It is to be hoped that excavation will reveal further structures of this type and that it will then be possible to establish their original function.

It was one of the special attractions of the Roman towns that they offered their citizens such amenities as places of public entertainment (theatres and amphi-theatres) and large public baths *(thermae)*. The theatres and amphitheatres of Gaul are of types peculiar to the province, no doubt related to the particular forms of entertainment preferred by the local inhabitants. Theatres of the regular Roman type, as at Orange *(Plate 77)*, Arles and Vaison, and amphitheatres of classical type, as at Nîmes *(Plate 80)* and Arles, are found only in southern Gaul and at Lyons. In the Three Gauls, in the small sanctuary townships and even in towns of some size, various hybrid forms are found—combined theatres and amphitheatres, theatres with an arena, half-amphitheatres, amphitheatres with a stage, as at Grand *(Plates 128, 131)* and Paris. Compromises of this kind seem to reflect the preferences of the provincial public, who were particularly fond of processions, pantomimes and spectacle plays, and also liked to attend perfor-mances of religious mysteries. Some of these theatres (Augst, Champlieu, Aven-ches) are directly associated with a neighbouring sanctuary, of which they appear to be a kind of annex.

The ancient buildings which have left the largest and most spectacular remains are undoubtedly the public baths. Every town of any size possessed at least two such establishments, sometimes three. Most of them seem to be no earlier than the end of the 2nd century, when the large symmetrical *thermae* came into favour. The oldest baths of this type may be those in the Metz museum, which recent excavations have allowed us to date to the reign of Trajan. There were, however, other baths in Metz of still earlier date in the Rue des Clercs; these date from the 1st century, although the complete plan has not yet been recovered.

The largest and best preserved of all are the *thermae* of Trier—the baths of Sainte-Barbe, which can be dated to the 3rd century, and the large Imperial Baths built in the reign of Constantine. The Imperial Baths had a somewhat chequered career: designed and built for use by the Emperor and the court, they remained unfinished after Constantine's departure and were never used in their original form.

Associated with the baths were the aqueducts and water supply pipes of which some considerable remains have survived, like the Pont du Gard and the aqueduct of Jouy-aux-Arches, near Metz *(Plates 78, 79, 81)*. The provision of an adequate water supply was one of the Romans' major concerns, requiring considerable engineering skill, the execution of immense building operations and a complete administrative infrastructure. Many ancient towns, including Rome itself, were unable to survive the destruction of their aqueducts. A. Audin has shown that the collapse and abandonment of the upper town at Fourvière was a consequence of the cutting of the aqueducts which supplied it with water, and which seem to have been out of use by the end of the 3rd century.

The Mania for Building

After this rapid survey of town building in Gaul we can hardly avoid mention of a problem which must occur to any reasonable observer when he considers some of the archaeological evidence in the light of the historical record. Many buildings revealed by excavation, some of them of considerable size like the public baths, seem to have been little used or to have been converted almost immediately to serve some quite different purpose from that for which they were designed. Some buildings, indeed, were destroyed almost immediately after they were built.

How are we to assess the real utility or benefit of this orgy of building in a country which was not accustomed to such grandiose structures and had no real use for them? How could they be economically justified? May it not be that the heavy burden which their building and maintenance imposed on the taxpayer played a part in aggravating the financial crisis which was one of the reasons for the fall of the Empire? Surely this mania for building, and for building on such a vast and extravagant scale, must have weakened Roman society and made it incapable of reacting rapidly and effectively in times of crisis? Certainly it paralysed that society, for it locked up vast resources and immense capital investment in enterprises of very doubtful utility. It turned the Gallo-Roman towns into fragile organisms whose very existence might be threatened by the mere cutting of a lead pipe or the destruction of a bridge.

Economic Life

The vanity of all this building for display was soon driven home in the towns devastated by the invasions, when the inhabitants found themselves obliged to tear down with their own hands the marble facings and cornices in order to lay bare the main structures and re-use the stone in the construction of defensive walls. The towns now huddled within the narrow space enclosed by their ramparts. Only a city like Trier, now an Imperial residence, grew in size and erected large numbers of new buildings even more grandiose than the old ones.

It is paradoxical to observe how makeshift and poorly constructed were the industrial installations of Gaul, since it was industry that made the most substantial contribution to the economy of the country.

In L. Harmand's apt phrase, "Gaul was a great country which depended on manufacturing goods and selling them". The craftsmen of Gaul, with an inheritance of technical skills and traditions dating from the period of independence, were able to take full advantage of the Roman peace, Roman technical advances and the new markets which were now open to them within the Roman world. As a rule they plied their various trades on the outskirts of the towns, in suburbs or *vici* of poorly constructed buildings of timber and daub, rarely of stone, which grew up along the roads. These industrial townships consisted of groups of small workshops, and occasionally of large *villae*, like the one at Anthée near Namur, which were in effect self-contained factories. Some of the products in which the craftsmen of Gaul specialised—vases of tinned or silvered bronze, fibulas, sometimes decorated with multi-coloured enamels, glassware and pottery—found a ready market all over the Empire and made their way even into remote barbarian countries like Norway and Sweden.

Space does not permit a detailed discussion of the industries of Gaul, which were many and varied: the range included the manufacture of ironware—traditionally a flourishing industry in Gaul—spinning and weaving, the production of glassware and enamels, the leatherworking industries (including the manufacture of boots and shoes), basket-making, the wheelwright's trade, brewing and the foodstuffs industry (including in particular salt provisions). Special mention may, however, be made of two technical advances achieved by Gallic wheelwrights—

the wheeled plough and the earliest reaping machine, the *vallus*, which is referred to by Palladius and Pliny and is depicted in carvings found at Reims, Trier, Arlon and Buzenol.

The Production of Terra Sigillata

There is one industry whose products are of sufficiently distinctive character and have been sufficiently studied to allow us to sketch out their development over a period of time—the manufacture of the pottery known as *terra sigillata*. The shapes, the different quality of finish produced in the various workshops, the stamps used to produce the relief decoration, the signatures of the potters—all these characteristics help us to classify this ware according to the different workshops and periods. Many scholars in France and in other countries have contributed to our knowledge of *terra sigillata*, which is increasing year by year and constantly gaining in precision and objectivity. The recent discoveries in which the present author has been concerned, particularly the Boucheporn excavations, are opening up quite new historical perspectives.

One significant point should be noted at the outset: this is one field in which the craftsmen of Gaul quickly succeeded, after a brief apprenticeship, in equalling their Roman masters and indeed in ousting them from their established markets. In the reign of Augustus, from about 30 B.C., Italian potters produced a fine ware with an orange-coloured fabric and a sealing-wax-like red glaze which achieved wide popularity in all the markets of the Mediterranean world, in Spain, in Gaul and in Roman Germany. This pottery, produced at Arezzo and Pozzuoli and called *terra sigillata*, was in fact the latest expression of the Campanian pottery of Hellenistic origin from which it was directly derived; but while the Campanian ware was fired in reducing conditions and had a violet-blue glaze with a metallic lustre the *terra sigillata* was fired in oxidising conditions and had a handsome red slip. It was sometimes plain, sometimes with a moulded decoration of delicately executed reliefs, frequently of high artistic quality. The potters often signed their work, and some of them, like Tigranes and Pantagathus, were true artists.

The pottery produced in Arezzo turns up constantly in Gaul, in the earliest Roman camps in Germany (Oberaden, Haltern), in the *oppida* of the Early Gallo-Roman period (Gergovia, Bibracte) and in the earliest levels of the Roman towns: it is the only fine pottery of this type until about 10 A.D. At the same time certain potters in Cisalpine Gaul, like Aco or Acastus, were producing ware of a coarser fabric and with a less brilliant glaze—goblets decorated with rows of raised points and a variety of other patterns.

Even before the end of Augustus's reign, about 10 A.D., the technique of producing *terra sigillata* had been transplanted to Gaul. Its manufacture required long experience and a high degree of technical mastery, involving the use of a special slip, obtained by decanting the coarsest particles of clay and forming a colloidal paste with the finer particles, and a high-temperature firing in oxidising conditions in specially constructed kilns. Three groups of workshops were opened in Gaul at almost the same time—at La Graufesenque in the territory of the Ruteni (southern Gaul), at Lyons and in the Allier valley.

The potters of La Graufesenque and Montans learned the Roman technique and created a new style of their own, based on a fairly free imitation of the decorative style of Arezzo. The products of their workshops were of high quality, with a more brilliant red glaze and a harder paste, and were an immediate success in the markets of the Rhineland. At the same time the potters of Arezzo and northern Italy were establishing branch workshops at Lyons, whose products were of indifferent quality but strongly influenced the potters of central Gaul, then just setting up in business. At Lezoux, Coulanges and elsewhere the local potters produced slavish copies of Italian decorative patterns, obtained by taking moulds from originals. The vessels they produced still had a soft and friable paste and a washed-out pale pink slip. Their customers were mainly local, though some of their products have been found on sites in Roman Germany. No doubt this rising industry suffered a setback as a result of the events of the year 21. Production continued, however, during the reign of Claudius, showing a distinct improvement in the quality of the product and the standard of decoration but still following the traditions of Arezzo in decorative motifs and style (Atepomarus). The potters of La Graufesenque also continued to flourish in the reign of Claudius, maintaining their high standards and exporting their ware in considerable quantities to Germany and the recently conquered province of Britain.

The reign of Nero was a turning point in the development of the industry, when great changes took place in the style of decoration. In the early years of the reign the potters of La Graufesenque were influenced by the free and naturalistic style of ornament then becoming popular in the toreutic art (jewellery and ornaments) of the region, and began to use decorative motifs derived from the vine—vine leaves treated realistically, bunches of grapes, vine tendrils. It was at the end of

214

Nero's reign, however, about 60 A.D., that the decisive changes took place. A master potter named Germanus *(Plates 193, 194)*, notable alike for his technical ingenuity and his business capacity, brought in an entirely fresh repertoire of decorative themes borrowed from sculpture and introduced a new style of markedly indigenous character which became an immediate success. The potters of La Graufesenque now went on from strength to strength, taking over the workshops at Lezoux, introducing their own repertoire and their own style, and thus revitalising a centre of production which had fallen back into somnolence and obscurity.

A group of craftsmen from La Graufesenque and Lezoux set up a kind of pilot establishment at Boucheporn in the Moselle valley, an experimental workshop designed to acclimatise the technique of *terra sigillata* in north-eastern Gaul, with the idea of bringing production closer to their clientele, which consisted largely of the garrisons of the camps in the Rhineland. Between 60 and 70 A.D. this establishment produced *terra sigillata* closely imitating the ware produced at La Graufesenque—so closely, indeed, that it could not be distinguished from the genuine article were it not for the "wasters" rejected by the local potters which have been found in rubbish pits.

The Periods of Mass Production

About 70 A.D. a new type of vase, hemispherical in shape and with relief decoration, which could be produced more easily and more rapidly, was developed at La Graufesenque. This replaced the carinated vase (Type 29 in the classification established by the German archaeologist H. Dragendorff), having the double advantage over that type of being made from one piece of clay and requiring only a single mould. The vessels now produced at La Graufesenque also had a base formed of an applied ring moulding instead of a separately turned foot, a further simplification which made for more rapid production. The workshops established in the Moselle area before 70 A.D., however, still maintained, even for the hemispherical type of vase, the tradition of using moulds with considerable indentations in the base and separately turned feet—features which prove the earlier date of their establishment. Largely as a result of the greater ease of manufacture resulting from the introduction of the new hemispherical vase, the potters of La Graufesenque increased their output still further and went over to mass production, distributing their products on a vast scale all over the Empire. A consignment of pottery from La Graufesenque, still in its original crates, was found at Pompeii, buried under the ashes of the eruption of 78 A.D. It included both carinated vases of Dragendorff's Type 29 and hemispherical vases of Type 37.

Under the Flavians, about 80 A.D., a remarkable new potter named Saturninus arrived at Boucheporn, probably coming from southern Gaul (perhaps from the territory of the Ruteni and Gabali). He gave a fresh lease of life to the workshops of north-eastern Gaul, renewing their decorative repertoire by borrowing largely from sculpture and ornamental art, and also introducing mass production. He was associated with a group of Arvernian potters from Martres-de-Veyre near Clermont-Ferrand, where a new style was developed in the Flavian period. This combined decorative features from central and southern Gaul and made abundant use of patterns of great fineness and delicacy copied or moulded from the dies used in the production of metal ornaments. The potters who introduced this new style have been identified as the "potter of the shield and helmet", the "potter of the Cupids", the "potter of the gladiators" and the "potter of the rosette"; and some of them, like Ranto or Rantus and Drusus, are known by name.

About 90 A.D. a large new pottery workshop was established at Heiligenberg in the Bruche valley, near Strasbourg. The first potter working here, "Master F" (from the initial with which he signed his work), was a fairly slavish imitator of the decorative patterns of southern Gaul.

The reigns of the Flavian Emperors saw the workshops of southern Gaul at the peak of their expansion. In the meantime a large new workshop had been established at Banassac (Lozère), producing large quantities of pottery, though of inferior quality to the output of La Graufesenque. The lines of the relief decoration tend to be blurred, probably because the slip was applied with a sponge. This ware nevertheless shared in the vogue for the pottery of southern Gaul, which was exported in considerable quantities to Germany, Britain and the Danube area. Soon, however, the large scale of production led to a decline in artistic quality, which can be observed in the output of all the workshops, and particularly La Graufesenque. The decoration of the pottery was now clumsy, carelessly designed and slovenly in execution.

From the beginning of the 2nd century the different groups of workshops, whose style had been relatively uniform as a result of the movements of individual potters and the transfers of establishments which took place between 60 and 80 A.D., began to show marked divergences and to develop their own distinct personalities.

This process of differentiation began at Lezoux, where at the very end of the 1st century, between 90 and 100, we find a new school of inventive potters, with Libertus and Butrio at their head, enlarging the repertoire and rejuvenating the style of pottery by borrowings from the art of ornamental metalwork, and introducing the human figure as the predominant feature of their designs. At the same time new connections were being established between Lyons, where the technique of appliqué relief decoration was practised, and Lezoux, which copied this new technique from Lyons, the appliqué ornaments being moulded separately and stuck on to the vase with the aid of barbotine. These developments produced a transformation in style and decoration. Meanwhile the increasing popularity of *terra sigillata* seems to have led to the establishment of large numbers of new workshops in the first half of the 2nd century, both in the Allier valley and in north-eastern Gaul. While the workshops of southern Gaul continued with their mass production methods, with a steady decline in quality, the potters of central and north-eastern Gaul showed some consciousness of individuality and were more concerned with the artistic quality of their products.

About 90 A.D. Saturninus was joined by another potter named Satto, probably a native of Germany or one of the neighbouring cities, and the two of them developed a considerable business, establishing new workshops at Chémery about 90, at Blickweiler about 100 and at Mittelbronn about 140. Although the vases still bear a potter's signature, this is probably the trademark of a firm which would continue in existence after the deaths of the original founders. About the year 100 a number of native potters began to work at Boucheporn with Saturninus, Satto and the group of Arvernian potters. The Boucheporn workshop was still an experimental and training establishment at which new techniques were tried out and developed, and to which journeymen came to improve their skills and attain the status of master craftsmen. A new workshop was established at Luxeuil about 90 A.D., another at La Madeleine, near Nancy, some ten years later, and others again at Ittenwiller about 110, in the Argonne area between 100 and 120, and at Haute-Yutz and Trier about 130. One of the latest of these new establishments, the workshop founded at Rheinzabern between 130 and 140, quickly gained a lead over the others by its dynamism and industrial efficiency. Potters from neighbouring workshops whose sales were hit by competition from the new establishment flocked to Rheinzabern about 150; and a major industrial concentration thus grew up in the Palatinate, in striking contrast to the scatter of small workshops which had been the pattern at the beginning of the 2nd century.

After a temporary disturbance caused by the Germanic incursions in the reigns of Marcus Aurelius and Commodus the transfers of workshops and the movements of potters were resumed at the end of the 2nd century, and new establishments were set up in the *Limes* zone and the Danube valley. At Trier the artistic standard of the product was improved about 160 by the potters Censor and Dexter, who enlarged their repertoire with new themes taken from sculpture and ornamental metalwork (the Iphigenia cycle). Thereafter the production of *terra sigillata* with relief decoration continued until the middle of the 3rd century, gradually declining in technical competence and stylistic individuality.

A study of the distribution of the pottery produced by the different workshops in Gaul brings out a number of points with an important bearing on the economic history of the province. The main distribution centre for the pottery of Arezzo and northern Italy was Lyons, from which it travelled along the roads laid out by Agrippa. The pottery of southern Gaul passed mainly along the roads of Aquitaine and Germany and through the Rhineland. The pottery of Lezoux, on the other hand, seems to have found its main markets in western Gaul and to have been transported mainly along navigable rivers and waterways. But it also found its way to more distant markets in the East, for sherds of this ware have been found at Antioch on the Orontes; and the pottery of Lezoux, along with that of Martres-de-Veyre, was particularly popular in Britain. The output of Satto and Saturninus was mainly exported to the northern part of the *Limes* and to Britain; little of this ware found its way into the interior of Gaul. The pottery produced at Heiligenberg was mostly exported to the east (the southern part of the *Limes*, the Agri Decumates, Switzerland and the Danube valley); vases bearing the signatures of Heiligenberg potters have been found as far away as Poland. From the middle of the 2nd century the workshops of the Moselle and Argonne valleys sent their products mainly towards the west, transporting them by boat along the rivers, while the workshops on the Rhine (Rheinzabern) found their markets to the east.

By the 4th century the *terra sigillata* with relief decoration had disappeared, to be replaced by another ware of the same type with rouletted patterns, in a tradition going back to the days of Gallic independence. This pottery, which was produced in very large quantities in the workshops of the Argonne, is predominant in all deposits of the late Gallo-Roman period in northern and north-eastern Gaul. In southern Gaul its place is taken by a type of grey pottery with recessed decoration produced by stamping (the so-called "Visigothic" ware).

Glassworking (Plates 195–207)

Although glass objects are more difficult to recognise and classify than pottery, the excellent work done by Morin-Jean and a number of German scholars has made it possible to trace the history of the glass-making industry in Gaul from the 1st to the 4th century.

In the first century glass was imported from northern Italy and glassware of a greenish or bluish hue was manufactured in the Rhône valley. Vessels of coloured glass, some of them of high quality, were made in Cisalpine Gaul and brought into Gaul proper by way of the Alps and Switzerland; the cemeteries of Ticino have yielded considerable quantities of this ware.

In the 2nd century a number of glass-making shops were established in the Rhineland and Normandy, producing rather clumsily fashioned vessels, some of which can be distinguished by their characteristic shapes and by the makers' stamps (e.g., the barrel-shaped bottles known as *Merkurflaschen*).

At the end of the 2nd and beginning of the 3rd century the glass-making industry in Gaul was transformed by the settlement of some Syrian glass-makers at Cologne. The fresh impulse which they gave to the industry led to the establishment of a number of important new workshops producing glassware of very high quality which rapidly found markets throughout the Roman Empire. The glass-workers of Cologne produced various special kinds of glass, in particular an absolutely clear glass obtained by the use of manganese, glass decorated with threads of barbotine, multi-coloured glass and glass with engraved decoration. The development of the glass-making industry and the popularity of its products in the 3rd century led to the setting up of numerous new workshops in northern, north-western and north-eastern Gaul; and there were also glass-making establishments in Normandy and Belgium and all over the Rhineland.

From the 4th century onwards technical standards degenerated and the glass was coarser and less pure, with bubbles and "cords". New decorative techniques were introduced—lattice patterns, studs of coloured glass, and so on. Nevertheless the craftsmen still maintained a high degree of skill until about the middle of the 4th century, and some of their products (*diatretae*, articles of cut glass) are marvels of ingenuity and dexterity. After the closing of the Cologne workshops in 352 the glassware produced in Gaul was of much more variable quality and much less refined. A number of important workshops, however, continued the Roman traditions in Gallia Belgica into the early Middle Ages, their products being found in 5th century tombs and in burials of the Merovingian period.

Gallo-Roman Commerce

The history of Gallo-Roman commerce has still to be written, but we can at any rate attempt to sketch out the broad lines of its development. The class of businessmen *(negotiatores)*, with their dynamism and wealth, represented an important element in the life of Gaul. At first sight it is surprising to find how few high officials of the Empire were recruited in Gaul, in striking contrast to certain neighbouring provinces (Africa, Illyria), but the explanation is quite simple: the members of the Gallic aristocracy preferred the assured profits of trade to the uncertainties of a military or administrative career.

We can get a vivid impression of the life of the merchants of Gaul from the considerable numbers of carved funerary monuments to be seen in numerous museums from Narbonne and Bordeaux to Trier. The most important and the most informative of these come from the Moselle valley, and the best preserved of them all, still *in situ*, is the one at Igel, on the frontier between Luxembourg and Germany. The Secundinii, to whom this mausoleum belonged, were cloth merchants, and the scenes carved on the monument depict the various aspects of their business—the transport of large bales of cloth by river and by road, buying and selling in spacious shops, and scenes from the merchants' domestic round, including family meals at which the farmers contributed their quota to the feast.

A scene which recurs frequently in the carvings on monuments of this kind, of which substantial fragments have been discovered near Trier and Arlon and at Neumagen, is one showing farmers paying their rent *(Plate 176)*. This indicates that traders who had made a fortune in business preferred to put their money into land, and no doubt spent part of their time on their country estates; evidently, therefore, a class of rich landed proprietors had grown up by the 2nd century.

We shall consider two branches of commerce in particular, the wine trade and the cloth trade, since these are the trades most fully documented in the inscriptions and the monuments: apparently the wine dealers and cloth merchants were the most prosperous and successful of the businessmen of Gaul.

The wine trade was an old established one in Gaul, going back to the 6th century B.C., when the first Greek amphoras reached the valleys of the Seine, the Saône and the Danube. We have already noted that the trade was particularly active in southern Gaul from the end of the 3rd century B.C. The wine amphoras produced in Campania found their way into all the *oppida* of Gaul in the course of the 2nd and the 1st centuries B.C., and the trade developed on a still larger scale under the Empire, particularly when the Roman army was permanently stationed on the Rhine and, later, along the *Limes*. With the help of the inscriptions and the amphoras which have been discovered we can follow the transport of wine along a well organised route, starting from Pozzuoli and continuing by way of Ostia, Fos and Arles to Lyons. Here it was stored in warehouses, and then continued on its journey to the Rhine valley by way of the Saône and Moselle valleys and Trier, which was also an entrepôt and distribution centre. Thus we see that over most of the distance from Campania to north-eastern Gaul the wine amphoras were transported by water.

The cloth and wool trades, on the other hand, used the overland route for transport between the sheep-rearing areas, mainly in south-western Gaul, and the centres of production of certain special types of cloth and garments, mostly situated in the territory of the Santones and at Trier. The regular route ran from Bordeaux by way of Saintes, Sens, Reims and Arlon to Trier, Reims and Trier apparently being the main distribution points. No doubt there were large weaving establishments in northern Gaul and Belgium.

We may note also that the imported articles found in burials of the Imperial period in independent Germany mostly came from Gaul and had been manufactured there; and in carrying on this trade with Germany the businessmen of Gallo-Roman times were continuing a tradition which went back to the period of independence. A further market was opened up when Britain was incorporated in the Empire in the reign of Claudius, and the new province soon became one of the best outlets for the trade and industry of Gaul.

The Arts of Gaul

The sculpture of Gaul owed a great deal to the technical skills and artistic influences it received from Rome, though we must not underestimate the part played by the native temperament on the one hand or by Hellenistic and Oriental features which reached Gaul without passing by way of Rome. Had it not been for these contacts with Rome the art of Gaul, thrown back on its own resources and exposed to the influences which played on it in the normal way, would have become a kind of prefiguration of Romanesque art.

The Development of Sculpture

On the eve of the Roman conquest Gallic sculpture was already undergoing a transformation which was bringing it closer to the realism and humanism of the Greeks and Romans, though without losing any of its distinctive characteristics. Once Gaul came within the Roman orbit its regional sculpture passed through a number of successive phases, which may be briefly summarised as follows:

1. In the first phase we find a consciously created sculpture imported from abroad co-existing with a native popular style which still shows archaic features.

2. In the second phase we see the emergence of a provincial school of sculpture of some individuality, developed by native artists who have assimilated, in a manner personal to themselves, the teachings and the models received from Rome. This provincial sculpture then goes through a process of development, following the general trends prevailing in the Roman Empire.

3. In the third phase this provincial style degenerates, while a popular style derived from it branches off and follows a separate line of development influenced by native traditions.

This cycle was completed in Gaul between the reign of Augustus and the end of the 3rd century, and it was about to begin again when the Germanic invasions interrupted the development of Gallo-Roman art in the 4th century.

In the 1st century B.C. the art of sculpture in Provence produced such diverse works as the bas-reliefs on the mausoleum at Saint-Rémy, the funerary portraits of Republican date at Nîmes, the latest works of sculpture produced at Entremont *(Plates 46, 47)* and the man-devouring monster of Noves *(Plates 46, 47)*.

133, 134

141

142

143

144

145   146

147

48

49

51

150

By the reign of Tiberius a synthesis was being achieved in Gallia Narbonensis. A vigorous and individual school of sculpture existed at Arles, Avignon and above all at Orange, as exemplified by the bas-reliefs on the Orange triumphal arch *(Plates 132–134)*, combining a proper understanding of the principles of composition of Greco-Roman art with a realistic, tumultuous and romantic temperament which is very characteristic of the native plastic art of Gaul and differentiates it sharply from Roman art of the same period.

The archaic art of this period in the rest of Gaul is still partly attached to Gallic traditions and has not yet shaken off the clumsiness of the apprentice craftsman. In the bas-reliefs on the pillar erected by the boatmen of Paris, now in the Musée de Cluny *(Plate 138)*, the imitation of Roman models is still a little maladroit, while the scenes reflecting a native Gallic inspiration are of remarkable quality. In the reign of the Emperor Claudius there developed in Gaul, and particularly in the north-eastern part of the country, a notably successful synthesis between native traditions and Italic influences, coming this time not from Rome but from Cisalpine Gaul and in particular from Aquileia *(Plates 109, 111, 135, 139, 169)*. The hieratic and decorative style thus evolved foreshadows some aspects of Romanesque art. It is particularly well represented in Roman Germany and the neighbouring cities, in the territory of the Mediomatrici, the Treveri and the Lingones.

Just as in the reign of Nero, about 60 A.D., a first wave of influences from southern and central Gaul reached the potters' workshops of north-eastern Gaul, so at the same period the art of sculpture in bronze and stone was strongly influenced by the florid Baroque style of Gallia Narbonensis, which took on a specifically regional aspect in the Rhineland. The Jupiter Column of Mainz, erected in 66 A.D. by the *canabarii* of the city and decorated with sculpture by Samus and Severus, sons of Venicarus, shows how thoroughly these Gallic sculptors had assimilated this first contact with Hellenistic art in the reign of Nero *(Plate 137)*.

Under the Flavian Emperors the flow of influences from the south became more marked and more specific, particularly at Trier, where our investigations have revealed the activity of a team of sculptors from Gallia Narbonensis who had evidently migrated to the Moselle valley, in the territory of the Treveri, and were responsible for a number of funerary monuments and a triumphal arch celebrating the victory of Vespasian's forces in 70 A.D. over the Gallo-Germanic rebellion of the Civilis brothers, Tutor and Classicus.

The Richness and Variety of Provincial Art

From the beginning of the 2nd century influences from Rome and Italy ceased to play any part in the provincial art of Gaul, being replaced by direct Hellenistic influences—by the teaching, example and inspiration of foreign artists, sculptors and ornamental metalworkers attracted to Gaul by the wave of town building. These teachers seem to have found ready disciples, and their influence continued to be felt throughout the reigns of Trajan, Hadrian and the Antonines.

Thus while Gallo-Roman provincial art was represented until the end of the Flavian period by a style of sculpture which can be called Italo-Gallic, from the time of Trajan onwards it becomes Greco-Gallic. The impressive body of work found at Sens, Trier *(Plates 154, 155, 156)* and elsewhere bears witness to the activities and the influence of the Hellenistic sculptors and ornamental metal-workers, which can also be observed on the *sigillata* pottery produced in the time of Libertus, Satto and "Master F". The intense hellenisation of Gallic art in this period is a complex phenomenon, a spontaneous and far-reaching process which is far removed from a mere slavish copying of models and stereotypes and leads to the development of a school of provincial sculpture which is Hellenistic in technique and spirit.

During the second half of the 2nd century new influences, coming this time from the East by way of the Danube valley along with the mystery cults of Cybele and Mithra, introduced a romantic and dramatic note into the provincial sculpture of Gaul *(Plates 162–164)*. At the same period, however, there appears in Lower Germany a curious hieratic style *(Plate 173)*, reminiscent of the hieratic sculpture of the Claudian period and probably derived from cult statuary in bronze. Mean-while the realistic vein which found favour in this period of rising economic prosperity came to the fore in funerary art and produced some authentic master-pieces. Taken as a whole, Gallic provincial sculpture of the 2nd century A.D. *(Plates 154–156, 162–180)* is an art of extraordinary variety and of incomparable liveliness and artistic quality. The large quantity of material discovered and the studies carried out in recent years have increased our understanding of this im-pressive artistic achievement, the significance of which in the cultural inheritance of the West can hardly be overestimated.

At the beginning of the 3rd century a neo-classical reaction *(Plates 140, 145, 146)* took place in eastern Gaul, in clear opposition to the overstatement and artificial grandiloquence of Severan art. In this period, too, the native school of popular sculpture *(Plates 181–183)*, which had come under the influence of the academic style and learned a great deal from it, branched off the main stem to produce an offshoot of outstanding vigour. This development was in a sense favoured by the tribulations to which Gaul was exposed during this century of military anarchy. The new style took over from the academic school of official sculpture, now impoverished and far gone in decay. The result was to produce some unexpected resurgences of Celtic trends *(Plates 112–114)*.

The cleavage which thus developed in the 3rd century between the decadent academic school of sculpture and the native popular style continued in the 4th century. The two movements of artistic renewal *(Plates 150–152)* which took place in the reign of Constantine and, after 352, in the reigns of Valentinian and Gratian were confined to certain areas and certain social groups. The gulf which now opened up between the aristocratic culture and eclectic art of the ruling classes and the increasingly barbarous style of the native arts grew steadily deeper, and all prospects of assimilation between the two were destroyed by the invasions and the spread of Germanic influence.

The influence of Roman art was a decisive factor in the growth of the provincial art of Gaul. Its contribution was of fundamental importance, both for the techniques it introduced and the models it offered for imitation. From this imported art the popular art of Gaul was, in the last analysis, derived, even when it was giving expression to native tastes and traditions; though we must not underestimate the importance of these traditions, nor of the Hellenistic and Oriental elements which were also thrown into the melting pot of Gallic provincial art.

THE RELIGION AND GODS OF GAUL

VII

The Effect of Romanisation on Native Religious Beliefs

I t was a basic fact of life in the ancient world, and particularly in the Roman Empire, that religion was inseparable from administration and politics. We must therefore consider to what extent the introduction of Roman religious ideas affected the native creeds and cults. Was the Gallic religion completely displaced, or did it merely undergo a surface change, remaining faithful in all essentials to its traditions?

The impact of Rome on Gallic religion took a variety of forms—the establishment of the Imperial cult, the psychological and propaganda effect of putting a special Roman interpretation on the Celtic gods, and the diffusion of the various Oriental cults. In the present state of knowledge it is difficult to achieve a complete and objective assessment of the influence of these various factors on the religion of Gaul: this chapter, therefore, will merely set out some tentative views based on the results of current research.

The Lyons Altar

The establishment of a provincial centre of the Imperial cult at Lyons was an act of high political and religious significance. The object was to enable the Gauls to take part directly and personally in the public worship of the goddess Roma and the heroised Augustus, rather than through the intermediary of officially appointed priests. The significance of this foundation must be assessed in the light of our knowledge of the historical situation and the findings of archaeology, taking account particularly of the new evidence made available by A. Audin's recent work. It now appears that the setting up of the Lyons altar was not in the same category as the establishment of the numerous *capitolia* in Gaul, like those at Vienne, Nîmes, Narbonne, Saint-Bertrand-de-Comminges or Toulouse. These were merely Roman sanctuaries built by the Roman authorities in accordance with Roman usages and rites; but the establishment, at the confluence of the Rhône and the Saône, of a sanctuary common to all the cities of Gaul represented a recognition of native politico-religious ideas and their reorientation to serve the ends of Roman religious policy. The traditional politico-religious gatherings of the Gauls, which Caesar tells us usually took place during the period of independence in the forest of the Carnutes, were now transferred to Lyons and put under the patronage of the goddess Roma and the *numen* or genius of the heroised Augustus.

This can be seen—to use a horticultural metaphor—as a process of grafting rather than transplanting, the Roman cult of Augustus and the goddess Roma being ingeniously grafted on to the traditions, customs and institutions of Gaul.

A. Audin rightly draws attention to the shape of the altar, which is known to us from its representation on the reverse of coins issued at Lyons *(Plate 102)* and from some remains of the structure which have survived (the syenite columns which were set on either side of the altar in the reign of Hadrian and fragments of the bronze wreaths held by the goddesses of victory who stood on top of the columns). This type of altar is not Roman; and the parallels cited by Audin suggest that it was a modification of a traditional native structure, a kind of portico like the one at Roquepertuse. The orientation of the window-like opening formed by the altar with the columns on either side was probably such that the sun appeared between the two columns on the day of the annual celebration (1st August) —an arrangement presumably of native origin. The 1st August was both the date of the great Celtic religious ceremony of Lugnasad and the day on which honour was paid to the *genius Augusti.*

The sanctuary area contained large porticoes laid out near a sacred spring, the main temple and a large amphitheatre—a layout similar to that of the great urban sanctuaries of native type like Augst or the sanctuary of Mars Lenus at Trier. All the evidence, therefore, points to a policy of merging the religious structures and rituals of Gaul into the official cult of Rome.

Interpretatio Romana and *Interpretatio Gallica*

This fusion was based on an idea which seems to have been familiar to the religious thought of the ancients—the conception of a real and deep-seated kinship between the different national religions of paganism. This idea, emanating originally from the Greek philosophers and in particular from the Pythagoreans, was taken over and used with great effect by the governing class which administered the Roman provinces, and was an important factor in the formation of a kind of religious syncretism of relatively uniform pattern throughout the Roman Empire.

This is the essential element in what has been called the *interpretatio romana,* the process by which the Romans put their own particular interpretation on the divinities of Gaul. The spirit in which the alliance between Gallic religion and the Roman cult at the altar at the Confluence was conceived throws a revealing light on this *interpretatio romana*, bringing out its full significance for Roman religious policy in Gaul. It enables us to appreciate the part played by religion in the Roman tactics of seeking a *rapprochement* between the peoples of Gaul and the people of Rome, in accordance with the Caesarean conception of the protectorate and the spirit of cooperation shown by some Gallic tribes, in particular the Haedui, in the early days of the conquest; and in this respect Augustus and his successors continued Caesar's policy.

Once the Romans were established in Gaul they promoted and directed the process of assimilation by which the gods of the Gauls were gradually merged into the divinities of Greece and Rome, and in this policy they found willing collaborators among the Gauls themselves and their priests, the druids. The Gallic religion found itself caught up in a system of equivalences, using all the resources of Greco-Roman symbolism, iconography and mythology to express its own myths and its particular beliefs. In other words the *interpretatio romana*, which the Romans saw as a Roman interpretation of the gods of Gaul, had its necessary and inseparable complement in an *interpretatio gallica*, a Gallic reinterpretation of Greco-Roman myths and symbols to express Gallic ideas. Here we come on the major difficulty which faces archaeologists and historians seeking to understand Gallic religion by reason of the very nature of the evidence on which they rely. Most of this dates from the Roman period, and at first sight seems to relate solely to Greco-Roman divinities or myths; yet I believe that these romanised images had a significance based on Gallic beliefs and traditions and can be interpreted by reference to Gallic mythology. It may be objected that we know nothing of Gallic religious beliefs or mythology. In fact, however, it is possible to reach the central core of Gallic religion and mythology by a series of comparisons between the imagery of the Gundestrup cauldron *(Plates 48–60)*, the most informative and illuminating piece of evidence we possess on Gallic religion during the period of independence, and that of the earliest known Gallo-Roman monuments, including in particular the Paris boatmen's pillar *(Plate 138)*.

Gallic Mythology

The mythological story which can be recovered by this means centres on a great mother goddess who marries first a sky god, Taranis, and then an earth god, Esus. The latter appears, according to season, either in human form or in the form of a monster who is half man and half stag, Cernunnos *(Plates 49, 52)*. As Esus he is the god of vegetation and, in spring, the mate of the mother goddess. As

Cernunnos he is the god of the underworld and of riches. At the end of winter he becomes the lover of the mother goddess, who leaves Taranis and his fearsome dogs to join him *(Plate 53)*. Esus's acolyte and protector, the hero Smertrius, kills Taranis's watchdog with the encouragement and help of the mother goddess, in a myth which recalls the Greek story of Heracles and Cerberus. The sky god, with the help of another dog, then takes his revenge by changing the mother goddess and her two attendants into cranes *(Plate 54)*. They are restored to human form by Smertrius, who achieves this by sacrificing the three divine bulls discovered by the Dioscuri *(Plates 55, 60)*. Finally the hero sacrifices a stag, thus enabling Cernunnos to return to earth in human form and marry the mother goddess.

On consideration of the accounts of pagan celebrations of calendar festivals which survived into the early mediaeval period (masquerades and dances in which men and women dressed up as stags and hinds) and of some French traditional folk customs I deduced that the Gauls held seasonal festivals every year to celebrate the main episodes in the myth, in accordance with an annual cycle. Thus the celebrations of the descent of the Mothers into the underworld linger on in certain local customs connected with the *réveillon* on Christmas Eve; the sacrifice of the stag and Esus's return to earth, celebrated in the early mediaeval period by masquerades and dances which were severely frowned on by the Church, still survive in the festivities, so pagan in spirit, of the Carnival. Even the sacred marriage of Esus after the sacrifice of the bulls, which is represented on the Paris boatmen's pillar, finds a remote reflection in the ceremonies of Mi-Carême as they were still celebrated at Paris in the 19th century.

I then saw that this new theory, linking much of French folklore and folk traditions with a distant past, threw a flood of light on some representations of Gallo-Roman religious themes which had hitherto remained obscure and unexplained. For example the theme of the bull with three cranes and Esus as a woodman *(Plate 138)*, which appears twice in the Gallic iconography of an early period, is readily explained by reference to the myth of the mother goddesses transformed into cranes for whom their future husband is searching in the forest and who perch on the bull which is to be sacrificed to restore them to human form. Similarly the representation of the "Saintes triad" *(Plates 118, 119)*, previously so enigmatic, is now easy to understand: the three bulls' heads surmounted by figures of a mother goddess, Hercules and Esus represent the changing of the cranes into mother goddesses after Smertrius had sacrificed the bulls in presence of Esus. The

154

155

157

162

167

172

178

179

central episode in the myth, the marriage of Esus, is depicted on the reverse side of the carved group, in which the god is shown holding the torc or nuptial necklace, ready to slip it round his bride's neck.

The Major Gods of Gaul

Two passages in ancient authors list for us the principal gods of the Gallic pantheon —a passage in Caesar about the five leading divinities (Jupiter, Mercury, Mars, Apollo and Minerva) and a reference in Lucan to the triad Esus-Teutates-Taranis. The glosses on the passage in Lucan written in Gaul in the 4th century establish equivalences between the Roman and the Gallic gods: for example Jupiter = Taranis; Mars or Mercury = Esus; Mercury or Mars = Teutates. These variations reveal the uncertainties of the *interpretatio romana*. An examination of the numerous monuments in which the people of Gaul gave expression to their collective piety, however, allows us to chart out the stages in the romanisation of the Gallic divinities and to observe the persistence of ideas based on the traditional mythology and the original triad of gods.

One of the earliest known representations of the three great gods of the Gauls appears on a silver goblet found at Lyons shortly before the last war *(Plates 122– 125)*. It depicts Teutates in the image of Mercury with a boar, associated with the crow which is the symbol of the Gallic Apollo. Taranis-Jupiter is represented by an eagle fighting a snake—an old symbol of the cosmic struggle between the celestial and the chthonian gods. Esus-Cernunnos is depicted in the form of a god holding a horn of abundance in his left hand and a torc in his right, lying on a couch and accompanied by a stag. No doubt this was the local version of the Gallic national triad, as worshipped in the Augustan period by the representatives of the Gallic cities assembled at the Confluence of the Saône and the Rhône.

The same triad is represented in a purely Gallic form by the divine group found at Euffigneix *(Plates 61, 62)*. A statue in the form of a tree trunk *(xoanon)* ends in a beardless head of Esus wearing a torc; on the trunk are two stylised eyes, the symbols of Taranis, the far-seeing god, and a boar, the usual symbol of Teutates. The same triad appears on the Rynkeby cauldron, which is decorated with the head of Esus wearing a torc, a small wheel with three curved spokes symbolising Taranis's wheel, and a boar, the symbol of Teutates.

The Development of the Gallic Pantheon

A series of dated monuments extending from Tiberius to Nero allows us to follow the evolution of Gallo-Roman religious iconography and to chart out the different stages in the development of the *interpretatio romana*. We observe a progressive assimilation of the gods of Gaul to the divinities of Greece and Rome and an apparent eclipse of the traditional images; but closer analysis reveals that under the outward semblance of the Greco-Roman gods the older divinities and the mythology associated with them, though now expressed by symbols borrowed from Greco-Roman mythology, still survive.

The Evidence of the Monuments

The pillar erected by the boatmen of Paris *(Plate 138)* is notable on the one hand for its representations of Gallic mythological scenes and native ceremonies (the bull with three cranes, Cernunnos, Smertrius, a procession of Gallic warriors bringing a votive torc to the mother goddess) and on the other for the figures of a number of Greco-Roman divinities which are either substituted for native divinities or associated with them in their original character (Mercury and Rosmerta, Apollo and Sirona, Mars and Ceres, a mother goddess and Fortuna). The pillar dates from the beginning of the reign of Tiberius (c. 17 A.D.).

The Mavilly pillar *(Plate 136)*, which dates from the beginning of Claudius's reign, marks a decisive advance in the progress of romanisation. It shows only Greco-Roman divinities, but these are depicted and grouped in such a way as to convey the substance of the great myths of the Gauls. One face of the pillar, showing Jupiter with one foot on a dolphin borne by Neptune, represents the rain myth, expressed elsewhere (e.g., on the Gundestrup cauldron) by Taranis throwing the wheel of fire *(Plate 48)*. The second face, with Vulcan and Venus in the upper part and Venus and Mars with a ram-headed snake in the lower part, represents the successive marriages of the mother goddess with the sky god and the earth god and the myth of the spring which welled up at the impact of the hammer cast down from heaven by Sucellus-Vulcan. The third face of the pillar represents the double aspect of the mother goddess, celestial in the guise of Fortuna, chthonian and funerary in the person of Proserpine holding a torch and snakes. The fourth face symbolises the divinatory and healing power of Apollo, who is attended by a winged genius in the form of Hercules with his club: the god is depicted bringing his prophetic and protective inspiration to the sanctuary, while a male figure—perhaps Esus returned from the underworld—rubs his eyes as if dazzled by the full light of day. The interpretation of this last scene, which differs from my earlier views, is the result of recent research, based particularly on comparisons with mythological scenes represented in the relief decoration of *sigillata* ware. The ornament on this pottery is now seen to be one of our most fruitful sources of information on the use of Greco-Roman symbolism to express Gallic themes. The Dijon pillar, which dates from the end of the reign of Claudius, represents a further step in the direction of romanisation. It shows a Mars of native type with a lance and ears of corn, probably the sidereal or celestial Mars identified by E. Thévenot, along with a Roman Hercules representing the Gallic hero Smertrius and a Juno who now replaces Ceres as a representation of the mother goddess.

The Ehrang stele *(Plates 141–144)*, which can be dated by its style to the reign of Nero, is the first appearance of a standard—almost a canonical—regional form of the group of principal divinities—Mercury, Hercules, Minerva and Juno. If we include Jupiter, who always appeared on a column on top of stelae of this type, we obtain a combination of the Capitoline triad (Jupiter, Juno and Minerva) with the Gallic triad of Jupiter–Taranis, Mercury–Teutates and Hercules–Smertrius. This new formula, which soon became general, seems to have been developed in Gaul by druids collaborating with the Romans but still preserving Gallic traditions. The highest pitch of romanisation is marked by the Mainz column *(Plate 137)*, which was dedicated in 66 A.D. On the base are figures of Mercury and Rosmerta, representing Teutates and his consort, Minerva and Fortuna, representing the two forms of the mother goddess, Jupiter–Taranis and Hercules–Smertrius. This last figure is accompanied by Bacchic masks, which seem to me to stand for Bacchus's train of revellers and also for the Gallic carnival. Support for this inter-pretation is provided by a large vase with relief decoration recently discovered at Alesia, which shows a troop of Bacchic revellers associated with a stag-hunting scene—clearly a reference to the annual ceremonies, including the sacrifice of a stag, and the masquerades which celebrated Esus's return to earth. On the stone cube above the stele with the figures of four divinities which forms the base of the Mainz column is a group consisting of Apollo and the Dioscuri which can be explained only on the basis of the Gallic myth I was able to deduce from a study of the Gundestrup cauldron: the Gallic Apollo joining with the Dioscuri and Teutates to protect the mother goddess in her conflict with Taranis–Jupiter and in her other tribulations. Among the allegorical figures of purely Roman origin on the column drums above the base we observe the figure of a mother goddess resting her foot on a bull's head, in evident allusion to the Gallic legend and to the ritual of the annual sacrifices in honour of the goddess.

In spite of the very advanced stage of romanisation to which the Mainz column bears witness it nevertheless shows a large number of characteristic associations which have no counterpart in Greco-Roman mythology and demonstrate the attachment of the priesthood and the people of Gaul to their native beliefs and rituals. Thereafter, in the 2nd century and during the period of Greek and Oriental influence in sculpture, we find Gallic religious ideas expressing themselves in three different ways: within a purely Greek and Roman system of expression, by associations between particular divinities or the representation of myths specially selected to refer to the Gallic triad or to stories from the Gallic legendary cycle; by specifically Gallic images; or by mixed groups of Greco-Roman and Gallic divinities.

The first method is represented by the pillar from Saint-Landry de Paris, now in the Musée de Cluny. This shows a sensual and romantic Venus holding a torch between her husband, Vulcan, and her lover, Mars—a clear allusion, as on the Mavilly pillar, to the successive marriages of the mother goddess with the sky god and the earth god.

As an example of the second type we take the Vendœuvres stele (now in the Châteauroux Museum), which also dates from the 2nd century. This shows on one face an Apollo–Belenus and on the face next to it a figure of Cernunnos attended by the Dioscuri trampling two ram-headed snakes underfoot. In this scene Divannos and Dinomogetimaros, the Gallic Castor and Pollux, are helping Cernunnos to return from the underworld, as in the myth which I identified on the Gundestrup cauldron.

The Reims stele exemplies the third type, the mingling of figures from Greco-Roman and Gallic mythology. It shows Cernunnos, wearing a stag's antlers on his head and squatting in the Gallic fashion, associated with a stag and a bull, and with a figure of Apollo on his right and Mercury on his left. The stag and the bull are the two victims which must be sacrificed to secure Esus's return to earth and the mother goddesses' resumption of human form; and the gods associated with Mercury and evidently giving him their support are the two gods who, in Gallic legend, side with Esus and the mother goddess in their conflict with Taranis. The allusion to Gallic tradition is clear.

The Evidence of Pottery Decoration

I have only recently observed that some of the scenes depicted in the decoration of *terra sigillata*, for which it has not been possible to suggest any interpretation in terms of Greco-Roman religion or mythology, are in reality strongly imbued with Gallic religious ideas.

We have already noted the meaning of the scenes depicted on the vase from Alesia, with its association between the train of Bacchic revellers and a stag-hunt. Another vase from La Graufesenque found in Britain shows a very unusual juxtaposition of themes from Greco-Roman mythology: a figure of Diana sacrificing a stag or a roedeer stands between a funerary Attis on the right and a figure of Victory holding a palm on the left, while in the upper register are a seated figure of Abundance and a figure of Leda with the swan. In the purely Greco-Roman system of mythology this association has no meaning; but if we accept a Gallic interpretation the whole thing becomes clear: the central scene represents the sacrifice of the stag and Esus's return to earth, which is assimilated to the resurrection of Attis and his victory over death. The representation in the upper register of the mother goddess in her two aspects as wife of the sidereal god (Leda and the swan) and of Esus (the figure of Abundance) is an allusion to the goddess's successive marriages with Taranis and Esus, associated with Esus's return to earth. Another vase from La Graufesenque belonging to the same period (reign of Nero) has as its principal decorative theme a fight between a lion and a boar *(Plate 193)*. This subject is certainly of religious significance, for it appears in a bas-relief in the sanctuary of Le Donon with the inscription BELLICO VS SURBUR, "To Bellicus, a votive offering from Surbur". On the La Graufesenque vases this theme alternates with a mask of Esus between two lions, accompanied by stags' antlers; the theme of lions pursuing a stag is also found. I would interpret these groups of animals as symbolising (a) the conflict between Taranis–Jupiter and Esus–Cernunnos (the lions and the mask of Esus, the lions and the stags) and (b) the fight between Teutates (the boar), who is defending Esus-Cernunnos, and Taranis (the lion).

Thus once again we are concerned with an allegory symbolising the mythological and cosmic struggle between the sky gods and the earth gods. As we extend our

275

understanding of the religious symbolism of Gallo-Roman art it is increasingly borne in upon us that these images of Greco-Roman gods and these stories from Greco-Roman mythology were used to express age-old religious ideas based on ancient native traditions. The religion of Gaul did not die out after the conquest: it merely changed its outward appearance, substituting the toga and the pallium for the breeches and the *sagum* of the Gauls.

The Assimilation of Oriental Religions

The Oriental mystery religions, and in particular the cult of Cybele and Attis *(Plate 165)*, found a fruitful soil for expansion in Gaul. The causes for this were complex, but among the main ones were the large Greek and Oriental elements in the population of the Rhône valley, particularly between Vienne and Lyons, and the movement of legionaries from the East or the Danube valley to the Rhine. Hitherto not enough attention has been paid, however, to another factor which undoubtedly contributed to the trend: the Gauls seem to have been disposed by their own religious beliefs and their native rituals towards the acceptance of religions which had certain points of contact and some striking similarities with their own.

The cult of Cybele *(Plate 90)* and Attis seems to have had its adepts in Gallia Narbonensis, the Rhône valley and the Rhineland by the 1st century A.D., to judge by the frequent occurrence of religious names relating to this cult and the representations of the funerary Attis on tombs. From the middle of the 2nd century, with the support of the Imperial authorities, Lyons became the main centre in Gaul of the cult of the Great Mother of the gods, and it was from here that the ritual of the *taurobolium* spread throughout Gaul. Gaul is in fact the province of the Empire which has yielded the largest number of taurobolic inscriptions.

It seems to me that one of the reasons for the popularity of the cult of Cybele in Gaul may have been a certain parallelism between the Oriental ritual and myths and the ceremonies of the native religion. The *arbor intrat*, the procession of Attis's pine-tree, had its counterpart in a Gallic rite in which warriors carried a tree in procession and then cast it into a pit. The custom is attested by a scene on the Gundestrup cauldron *(Plate 55)* and by the complete tree trunks, stripped of their branches and roots, which have been found in Gallic "funerary pits".

We have already noted that in scenes depicted on *sigillata* ware produced at La Graufesenque in the reign of Nero the resurrection of Attis was assimilated to Esus's seasonal return to earth. The *taurobolium*, too, had of course an approximate equivalent in the annual sacrifice of bulls in honour of the mother goddess. It seems likely that—even at Lyons itself—the cult of the Great Mother was to a considerable extent grafted on to a native cult of mother goddesses.

This is probably true also of the vogue for the cult of Mithra, some of the rites in which might seem to the Gauls to have affinities with their native religious rituals. Evidence of this is provided by a vase found at Lezoux, with appliqué reliefs in which the representation of Mithra slaughtering the bull is associated with a figure of a flute-player wearing a *nebris*, evoking the Bacchic revels and the Gallic carnival, and a seated figure of Abundance, recalling the great mother goddess of native tradition. This is another instance of the phenomenon we have already examined in our discussion of the *interpretatio romana*. The Gauls recognised the kinship between some of their myths and religious practices and the corresponding elements in the mystery religions of Oriental origin. This may have facilitated the expansion of these cults and made it easier for them to obtain converts; but it may also have led to the development of syncretisms between Celtic and Oriental cults similar to those we have already observed in the Gallic interpretation of the myths and divinities of Rome.

Survivals and Resurgences of Gallic Religion

At this point we are faced with a major question: did the introduction of Greco-Roman iconography and mythology on the one hand, and the rituals of Oriental cults on the other, represent a genuine conversion—that is, a profound transformation of the religious beliefs of Gaul?

An examination of the dated monuments, confirmed by the main historical sources and the evidence produced by excavation, seems to suggest the contrary. From the 3rd century A.D., even before the period of military anarchy, the Gauls appear to have returned to their earlier faith. The native gods, and in particular the figure of Teutates, long banished by the Romans, reappear in the inscriptions and on the figured monuments; and similarly the archaic figure of Taranis with his wheel begins to crop up again in the epigraphy and the iconography.

The Sanctuaries of Le Donon and Mackwiller

The excavations at Le Donon, the capital of the three confederated tribes of the Leuci, the Mediomatrici and the Tribocci, have yielded some valuable information on this point. The fifty or so figures of divinities discovered here included representations of four gods—the Gallo-Roman Mercury, carrying a purse and accompanied by a goat, a cock and a tortoise; Jupiter on horseback, with a snake-footed giant; Smertrius with a stag; and a naked god with a sword, undoubtedly representing the traditional figure of Teutates in his rôle as a warrior. The last of these figures dates from a late period (end of 3rd century), while the representations of the Gallo-Roman Mercury bear the stylistic characteristics of the 2nd century. The figure of Smertrius with the stag, recalling the sacrifice of a stag which brought about the resurrection of Esus and the ceremonies of the Gallic carnival, may be dated to the beginning of the 3rd century. The figures of Jupiter on horseback belong to the middle and end of the same century. It does look, therefore, as if the 3rd century was a period of return to the oldest religious traditions of Gaul.

This is confirmed by the excavations of the sanctuary of Mithra at Mackwiller, the remains of which were discovered in a quarry in the commune of Mackwiller in 1953. Although nothing was left but the foundations, in large blocks of sandstone, and the paving, a methodical excavation made it possible to establish that these were the remains of a temple in honour of Mithra and to follow the history of the structure. The site, which lay near a spring, had been sacred to the gods in the days of Gallic independence, and a shrine dedicated to the gods of the locality was established here by the 1st century. About the middle of the 2nd century the local landowner built a sanctuary in honour of Mithra; it was decorated with bas-reliefs, the largest of which depicted Mithra slaughtering the bull. On the plinth, and in an inscription of which a fragment was recovered, the native local divinity, Narius Intarabus, was associated with Mithra.

The sanctuary was partly destroyed at the end of the 3rd century, and in its place was erected a shrine in honour of the spring, re-using the existing blocks, some of them in a rather mutilated condition. The new sanctuary was built to a native plan, with one square structure enclosed within another and a basin in the centre of the inner cella for the spring. It thus appears that the period of Mithraic use was no more than an episode, lasting 120 or 130 years, in a much longer history. After the invasions of the 3rd century Mithra disappeared and an older Gallic god remained in sole occupation of the sanctuary which he had never wholly abandoned.

185

186

187

188

189   190

191

192

193

194

204

205

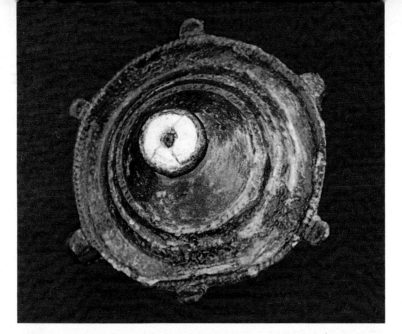

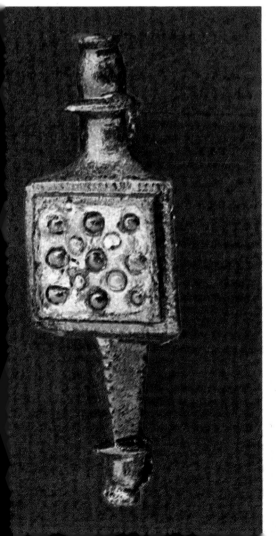

213

214

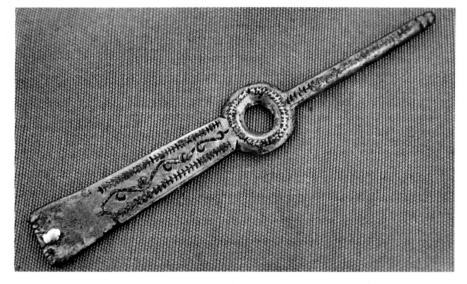

215

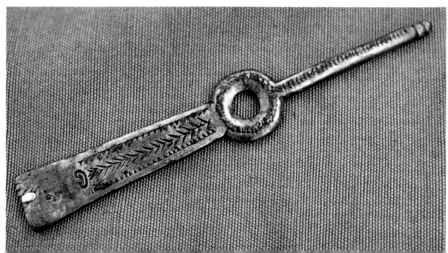

216

The history of this modest little sanctuary is thus not only instructive but symbolic The Greco-Roman and Oriental divinities may have been temporarily associated with the native gods; they may have overshadowed them; but they never totally destroyed them.

The Rôle of the Druids

The pattern of development which we have observed in the expression of Gallic religious beliefs—the progressive retreat, during the 1st and 2nd centuries, of the native divinities in their original form, and in particular of Teutates; the assimilation of the Greco-Roman pantheon, but at the same time the survival of the older traditions in imagery taken from Greco-Roman iconography and mythology; and then a sudden movement of resurgence from the 3rd century onwards—can be seen also in the history of the Gallic priesthood. The historical evidence on the druids shows that they were tolerated during the reign of Augustus so long as they were not Roman citizens, but persecuted by Tiberius and driven out in the reign of Claudius; they then made a comeback during the crisis of 70 A.D., when after the burning of the Capitol some of them foretold the fall of Rome and the transfer of power to the nations beyond the Alps (Tacitus, *Histories*, IV, 54). The story of Mariccus, a druid and prophet in the Gallic tribe of the Boii, who whipped up the ardour of his people in a rising against the Romans, shows that there were local centres of resistance (Tacitus, *Histories*, II, 61).

We hear nothing of the druids in the 2nd century, but they crop up again in the 3rd. We hear, for example, of prophecies directed against Alexander Severus and Maximinus (apparently emanating in the latter case from the druids serving Belenus-Apollo at Aquileia). During the same period the Roman Emperors themselves addressed their devotions to Gallic gods—Caracalla to the god of the springs at Baden-Baden, Diocletian and Maximian to the god Belenus of Aquileia.

The Emperor Constantine, before his conversion, had a pagan vision in a temple in Gaul, seeing himself in the form of an Apollo attended by a figure of Victory holding garlands who promised him a reign of thirty years. Following Grégoire and Piganiol, I interpret Constantine's "sign" as a pagan symbol: I see it as the Gallic symbol of an X, derived from Taranis's wheel, which would thus be the original source of the Constantinian monogram. Later the druids of Gaul seem to have tried to direct Constantine's pious aspirations towards Gallic forms of worship; and certainly Constantine himself seems to have been inclined, before his conversion, to turn towards certain forms of pagan syncretism.

299

The druids officially reappear in Gallic society in the 4th century. Ausonius mentions two famous druids in his *Commemoratio professorum Burdigalensium*; one of them called Attius Patera, a native of the city of the Baiocasses (Bayeux), the other called Phoebicius, an Armorican by origin (Ausonius, I, 1, IV, 7, and X, 22). One of Ausonius's ancestors, Arborius, who had taken part in the resistance against Victorinus at Autun in 269, has a religious name which may be an allusion to the Gallic myth of the tree with the three cranes perched in it.

Thus we see that the druids, after being persecuted in the 1st century and then relegated to obscurity during the period of Greek and Oriental influence, came to the fore again in the 3rd century, at the same time as the gods of Gaul were reappearing under their native names and in their original form.

The Persistence of Tradition

How are we to explain this long survival and these resurgences of the religion of Gaul? A number of different factors can be identified.

The first was the persistence, throughout all vicissitudes, of the Gallic priestly class, the druids. They were persecuted, no doubt, but not destroyed. No doubt, too, they were induced to accept a compromise with the Romans in the *interpretatio romana* of the Gallic divinities, but this was balanced by the important part they played in the *interpretatio gallica* of the Greco-Roman gods and myths, of which we have considered a number of examples. If the druids were able to stage a comeback in the 3rd and 4th centuries, at the same time as the divinities of Gaul were re-establishing their position, this was because they had been able to maintain the ancient Gallic traditions in the shadow of the great sanctuaries, some of which were dedicated to the native Apollo while others were gathering places or pilgrimage centres like the sanctuary at Le Donon. In the temples of Apollo, which were always situated at a spring, the rites of prophetic medicine and divination inherited from the Greeks were practised with the approval of the Romans. These were the main bastions of druidism and the religious resistance in Gaul, against which the Roman authorities were powerless.

There is still another reason for the survival of Gallic religion and customs—the existence of certain unassimilated areas outside the romanised territories in which the native traditions of Gaul were preserved and cherished. These might be mountainous districts such as were found in the Vosges, the Palatinate, the slate plateau of the Rhineland, the Massif Central and the Pyrenees, or purely agricultural districts like Normandy.

We can distinguish a number of features which contributed to the preservation of the native traditions in these pockets of Gallic nationalism within Gallo-Roman territory. The first was the maintenance of a settlement and farming pattern different from the regular Roman system: in place of the *fundus* there was a scatter of small hamlets. The second was the persistence of small closely-knit communities of villagers and craftsmen huddled round a sanctuary, a place of worship, or round a cemetery or burial ground, which was also a cult site.

These conditions were satisfied in Normandy, with the *fana* or small Gallic sanctuaries which have been studied by de Vesly; in the districts of Comminges and Couserans in the central Pyrenees, with their cemeteries situated round the sanctuaries of local gods; and in the Basses-Vosges, with their cemeteries adjacent to and associated with temples of Mercury. In the two latter areas the preservation of religious beliefs and the maintenance of burial practices went hand in hand, for the stele houses of the Pyrenees and Vosges are heirs to a long tradition which goes right back to the structures within the Bronze Age tumuli.

The period of semi-freedom at the beginning of the 1st century, when there was relatively little intervention by the Roman administration in the life of Gaul, undoubtedly made an important contribution to the preservation of native traditions. Later the rural exodus brought a movement of population from the farming and upland communities to the towns, where the incomers were merged with other population groups, including some from the East, which had traditions similar to their own; and these contacts led to the emergence of a curious syncretism to which Gallic traditions contributed their share.

Another sign of the survival of native customs is the very frequent occurrence in both rural and urban sanctuaries of a type of temple peculiar to Gaul, either square, polygonal or circular in plan. The origins of this type of structure are lost in the mists of the Gallic past, but the excavations of A. Brisson and A. Loppin have demonstrated its connection with the timber-built temples in honour of heroes or gods of the underworld which are found in association with funerary precincts from the La Tène period onwards.

Some of these sanctuaries stand by themselves in the open countryside, as in Normandy. Some are grouped in small sacred enclosures, as at Pesch in the

Rhineland. Others are in regular temple quarters containing considerable numbers of shrines, as at Trier and in the Altbachtal. Others again, as at Autun or Périgueux, are built within large Gallo-Roman cities and are among their most important buildings. It is in the religious field that the survival of Gallic traditions within the romanised provincial civilisation of Gaul is most striking and most clearly apparent.

CONCLUSION

I t is relatively easy to write a brief account for the general reader of the results achieved by archaeology in an entirely new field which has been explored only by trained archaeologists, as is the case with Crete or Iran. The results tend to be fairly spectacular; and the prospects opened up are so new, and the number of excavations and discoveries still so restricted, that a reasonably complete account of them can be given within a limited compass. But the archaeology of the countries of western Europe, and of Gaul in particular, is in very different case. It is made up of a great diversity of individual contributions to research and discovery, many of which have been published only in the most sketchy way. The problems are not simple in themselves, and have been complicated still further by years of discussion and dispersal of effort. The present work, therefore, is unduly long and still far from complete; and for this I must offer my apologies to the reader, who must also forgive me for so frequently citing my own work and putting forward personal views.

I have sought to show that only the application of proper archaeological methods, in particular stratigraphic excavation, supplemented by the various techniques of scientific analysis now available, offers the prospect of bringing order out of the often random and inconsistent results achieved by researches which have for so long been carried out in a haphazard and unorganised way. Nor must we overlook the need to build up the evidence from different fields into a synthesis, which alone will enable us to interpret the results of our research and suggest further lines of study.

I have also tried to show that excavation and discovery, however spectacular the results, are not ends in themselves. The conception of archaeology which I have put forward—a form of applied history, of "history on the ground"—involves a quest for Man through all the various manifestations of his activity, his spirit and mind through the works of art and the religious monuments he has left behind him, and the great vistas of the past through the countless clues which we find buried under the earth.

The main problem with which we are faced when we consider the antiquities of Gaul is the question of the continuity of Celtic Gaul throughout the development of Roman Gaul, the persistence of the native traditions in spite of romanisation. We have observed in the course of our survey that notwithstanding the adroit and often successful efforts of Roman policy and administration to assimilate them completely the Gauls—wearing Roman dress, living in the Roman way, speaking Latin, worshipping the gods of Greece and Rome and apparently converted to alien religions—nevertheless preserved many distinctive features of their own. In their provincial architecture, their art and their religious imagery we can recognise—sometimes preserved intact, sometimes concealed under the disguise of romanisation—the beliefs, customs, styles and structures which they had inherited from their remotest ancestors. Then, with the eclipse of Roman authority in the 3rd century the province, thrown back on its own resources, returned to its past, though still preserving the indelible imprint of *romanitas*.

In 4th century Gaul, as we learn from Sulpicius Severus, three languages were spoken—Latin, the language of Caesar and Cicero; Celtic, the language of Vercingetorix; and "Gallic", a provincial dialect spoken by the ordinary people which was a blend of popular Latin and Gallic elements. It was from this patois that, in due time, modern French was born.

The provincial civilisation of Gaul was thus a mosaic formed of surviving native traditions, elements contributed by the Romans, and Greek and Oriental influences, all intimately associated in a very varied and very personal pattern remarkable for its diversity of tone and colour. This is the pattern revealed to us by the study of the archaeology of Gaul.

CHRONOLOGICAL TABLE

Dates	Main chronological divisions	Dates	Important events
B.C.		B.C.	
1800–1500	Early Bronze Age	About 1500	Indo-European invasions; Proto-Celts in S. Germany and Eastern France
1500–1200	Middle Bronze Age	1250	First Proto-Celtic waves into Central and Eastern Gaul
1200–725	Late Bronze Age	1000	Large-scale Proto-Celtic invasions enter Gaul (Urnfields)
725–480	Hallstatt period	725	Thraco-Cimmerian incursions into Balkans
		600	Foundation of Marseilles
		500	First waves of Gallic invaders in Southern Gaul and Northern Italy
480–50	La Tène period	390	Second wave of Gallic incursions in Northern Italy
		334–326	Conquest of Alexander; first Gallic coins
		327–325	Voyages of Pytheas
		300	Advance of Germanic tribes into S. and W. Germany
		279–278	Celtic incursions into the Balkans and Asia Minor
		250	Belgic incursions into Northern Gaul
			Further Celtic incursions into Northern Italy
		122–118	Roman conquest of the *Provincia*
		58–50	Caesar's conquest of the Three Gauls
50 B.C.–10 A.D.	Early Gallo-Roman period	43	Foundation of Lyons and Augst by Plancus
		27	Accession of Augustus
		9 A.D.	Defeat of Varus

Dates	Main chronological divisions	Dates	Important events
A.D.		*A.D.*	
10–40	From Augustus to Claudius	21	Revolt of Sacrovir and Florus (in reign of Tiberius)
40–70	From Claudius to the crisis of 70	43	Beginning of conquest of Britain in reign of Claudius
		48	On the initiative of Claudius, the leading men of Gaul are granted the status of Roman senators
		50	Foundation of Colonia Agrippa and the colony of Trier
		68–70	Political crisis; civil and military risings
70–97	Flavian period, to the crisis of 97	71	Reorganisation of army by Vespasian
		74	Annexation of Agri Decumates; the first Limes
		83	Annexation of the Taunus and Wetterau; the Limes of Domitian
		88	Rising of Antonius Saturninus
		96–97	After murder of Domitian, crisis and destruction in Northern Gaul
97–120	Period of Trajan and Hadrian	120	Stabilisation of defensive line on Limes
120–190	Antonine period	160	Official cult of Cybele at Lyons
		170–190	First Germanic incursions into Gaul
		176	Persecutions of Christians in Lyons
190–235	From Commodus to the Severans	197	Defeat of Albinus and sack of Lyons
		212	Edict of Caracalla
		233–235	Germanic incursions into North-Eastern Gaul
235–275	Period of anarchy during the 3rd century	257	Collapse of the Limes and withdrawal to Rhine

Dates	Main chronological divisions	Dates	Important events
		259–260	Disturbances and invasions; beginning of Gallic Empire (Postumus)
		268–269	Siege of Autun by Victorinus
		273–274	End of Gallic Empire
275–306	First restoration, by the Illyrian Emperors and the Tetrarchy	276–282	Probus clears the barbarians out of Gaul; edict authorising the cultivation of vine in N.E. Gaul
		285	Trier becomes capital of Gaul
		286–289	Maximian's campaigns of repression against the Bagaudae
		296	Constantius Chlorus defeats rebellion in Britain
		296–306	Restoration of Gaul; establishment of German settlers
306–350	Second restoration, by Constantine and his successors	306–312	Constantine in Gaul; much building at Trier
350–357	Period of civil wars and invasions	350–352	Political and military crisis; invasion of N.E. Gaul
357–407	Third restoration (Julian, Valentinian and Gratian)	357	Julian, as Caesar, defeats the Alamanni near Strasbourg
		358–360	Restoration of Gaul by Julian
		363–367	Valentinian
		367	Gratian appointed Augustus; Trier once again becomes the capital
		370–397	St Martin preaching in Gaul
		388	Invasion of Gaul
		395–396	Headquarters of Prefecture of the Gauls transferred from Trier to Arles
407–451	Following the Vandal invasion of 406–407, final attempts at restoration; the end of Roman Gaul	406–407	Vandal invasion
		409	Reorganisation of the Rhine front
		411	Burgundii in the dukedom of Mainz
		425	Aetius in Gaul
		451	Attila's invasion; he is defeated and driven back (Campus Mauriacus, near Troyes)

SELECT BIBLIOGRAPHY

A. AUDIN, *Lyon, miroir de Rome dans les Gaules*, Paris, 1965.

F. BENOIT, *Mars et Mercure*, Aix, 1950.
— *L'art primitif méditerranéen de la vallée du Rhône*, Aix, 1955
— *Entremont, capitale celto-ligure des Salyens de Provence*, Aix, 1957.
— *L'épave du Grand Congloué à Marseille*, Paris, 1961.
— *Recherches sur l'hellénisation du Midi de la Gaule*, Aix, 1965.

A. BLANCHET, *Les enceintes romaines de la Gaule*, Paris, 1907.

A. BRISSON and J.-J. HATT, "Les nécropoles hallstattiennes d'Aulnay-aux-Planches", *Revue Archéologique de l'Est*, IV, 1953, pp. 193–233.

M. CLERC, *Massalia*, 2 vols, 1927 and 1929.
— *Aquae Sextiae*, 1921.

L. A. CONSTANS, *Arles antique*, Paris, 1921.

J. DÉCHELETTE, *Les vases céramiques ornés de la Gaule romaine*, Paris, 1904.
— *Manuel d'archéologie préhistorique et celtique*, 4 vols, 1927.

E. DELORT, *Vases ornés de la Moselle*, Nancy, 1955.

J. DE VRIES, *La religion des Celtes*, Paris, 1963.

M. M. DUVAL, *La vie quotidienne en Gaule pendant la paix romaine*, Paris, 1953.
— *Les dieux de la Gaule*, Paris, 1957.
— *Paris antique, des origines au IIIe siècle*, Paris, 1961.

H. P. EYDOUX, *Monuments et trésors de la Gaule*, Paris, 1958.
— *Lumières sur la Gaule*, Paris, 1960.
— *Hommes et dieux de la Gaule*, Paris, 1961.
— *Résurrection de la Gaule*, Paris, 1961.
— *L'histoire arrachée à la terre*, Paris, 1962.
— *La France antique*, Paris, 1962.
— *Réalités et énigmes de l'archéologie*, Paris, 1964.
— *Les terrassiers de l'histoire*, Paris, 1966.

A. GRENIER, *Manuel d'archéologie gallo-romaine*, 7 vols, Paris, 1931 to 1960.
— "La Gaule romaine", in *An Economic Survey of Ancient Rome* (ed. Tenney Frank), III, Baltimore, 1937.
— *Les Gaulois*, Paris, 1970.

J.-J. HATT, "De l'âge du Bronze à la fin du premier âge du Fer", *Bulletin spécial du cinquantenaire de la Société Préhistorique Française*, 1954, pp. 101–110; 1954, pp. 379–384; 1955, pp. 99–101 and 397–400; 1965, pp. 434–445; 1958, pp. 304, 305; 1961, pp. 184–195; 1963, pp. 659–667.
— *La tombe gallo-romaine*, Paris, 1951.
— *Strasbourg aux temps des Romains*, Strasbourg, 1953.
— *Histoire de la Gaule romaine*, Paris, 1966.
— *Inventaire des collections publiques françaises: sculptures antiques régionales, Strasbourg, Musée archéologique*, Paris, 1964.
— "Essai sur l'évolution de la religion gauloise", *Revue des Etudes Anciennes*, 1965, 1, pp. 80–125.
— *Sculptures gauloises*, Paris, 1966.

F. HERMET, *La Graufesenque*, 1934.

H. HUBERT, *Les Celtes*, 2 vols, Paris, 1932.

P. JACOBSTHAL, *Early Celtic Art*, Oxford, 1944.

J. JANNORAY, *Ensérune, étude des civilisations préromaines de la Gaule méridionale*, Paris, 1956.

R. JOFFROY, "La tombe de Vix", *Monuments et mémoires publiés par l'Académie des Inscriptions et Belles-Lettres (Fondation Piot)*, 1954.
— *L'oppidum de Vix et la civilisation hallstattienne finale dans l'est de la France*, Paris, 1960.
— *Les sépultures du Premier âge du Fer en France*, Paris, 1960.
— *Le trésor de Vix*, Paris, 1962.

W. KIMMIG, "Où en est l'étude de la civilisation des Champs d'Urnes en France?", *Revue Archéologique de l'Est*, II, 1951, 2, pp. 6–21; III, 1952, 1, pp. 27–75; V, 1954, 1, pp. 76–97, and 3, pp. 98–121.

Abbé B. LACROIX, *La nécropole préhistorique de la Colombine*, Paris, 1957.

P. LAMBRECHTS, *Contribution à l'étude des divinités celtiques*, Bruges, 1942.
— *Exaltation de la tête dans la pensée et dans l'art des Celtes*, Bruges, 1954.

J. LE GALL, *Alésia, archéologie et histoire*, Paris, 1963.

F. LEROUX, *Les druides*, Paris, 1961.

M. LOUIS and O. and J. TAFFANEL, *Le Premier âge du Fer languedocien*, 3 vols, Montpellier, 1955, 1958, 1960.

M. E. MARIEN, *Trouvailles du Champ d'Urnes et des tombelles hallstattiennes de Court-Saint-Etienne*, Brussels, 1958.

OSWALD and PRICE, *Introduction to the Study of Terra Sigillata*, London, 1920, reissued 1966.

A. PERRAUD, *Le Pègue, préface de Marseille*, Paris, 1956.

H. ROLLAND, *Fouilles de Saint-Blaise*, 2 vols, Paris, 1951 and 1956.
— *Fouilles de Glanum*, 2 vols, Paris, 1946 and 1958.
— *Glanum, Saint-Rémy-de-Provence*, Paris, 1960.

Nancy SANDARS, *Bronze Age Cultures in France*, Cambridge, 1957.

M. L. SJOESTEDT, *Dieux et héros des Celtes*, Paris, 1940.

J. A. STANFIELD and G. SIMPSON, *Central Gaulish Potters*, Oxford, 1958.

E. THEVENOT, *Les Gallo-Romains*, Paris, 1948.
— *Sur les traces des Mars celtiques*, Bruges, 1955.
— *Histoire des Gaulois*, Paris, 1960.

J. VENDRYES, *La religion des Celtes*, Paris, 1949.

F. VILLARD, *La céramique grecque de Marseille*, Paris, 1960.

P. WUILLEUMIER and A. AUDIN, *Les médaillons d'applique gallo-romains de la vallée du Rhône*, Paris, 1952.

P. WUILLEUMIER, *Lyon, métropole des Gaules*, Paris, 1953.

LIST OF ILLUSTRATIONS

23	Torc from Trichtingen, Württemberg. Silver. 4th century B.C. Stuttgart Museum. (Ph. Museum)
24, 25	Celtic oenochoe from Hallein, Austria. Bronze. 3rd century B.C. Salzburg Museum. (Ph. Museum)
26, 27	Arnoaldi Situla: Gallic and Etruscan soldiers. Bronze. Bologna, Italy. 5th century B.C. Civic Museum, Bologna. (Ph. Museum)
28	Torc from Filottrano. Gold. 4th century B.C. Ancona Museum. (Ph. Museum)
29	Torc from Rodenbach. Gold. 5th century B.C. Speyer Museum. (Ph. Museum)
30, 31	La Tène vases. Pottery. 5th century B.C. Epernay Museum. (Ph. J. J. Hatt)
32	Bird-shaped vase from Saint-Memmie. Pottery. 5th century B.C. Epernay Museum. (Ph. J. J. Hatt)
33	La Tène vase. Pottery. 4th century B.C. Epernay Museum. (Ph. J. J. Hatt)
34	Bull's head with knobbed horns. Provenance unknown. Bronze. 1st century B.C. Museum of National Antiquities, Saint-Germain-en-Laye. (Ph. J. J. Hatt)
35	Stylised human head. Cast of bronze original from Antheuil (Orne). 1st century B.C. Museum of National Antiquities. Saint-Germain-en-Laye. (Ph. J. J. Hatt)
36	Openwork ornament. From chariot tomb at Cuperly (Marne). Bronze. 4th century B.C. Museum of National Antiquities, Saint-Germain-en-Laye. (Ph. J. J. Hatt)
37	Gallic object decorated with studs of coral. From Saint-Germain-sur-Tourbe (Marne). 4th century B.C. Museum of National Antiquities, Saint-Germain-en-Laye. (Ph. J. J. Hatt)
38	Pillar from St Goar. 4th century B.C. Bonn Museum.
39	Oppidum of Entremont: Gallic houses. 2nd century B.C. (Ph. M. Giraud-Héraud)
40	Entremont: base of an oil mill. 2nd century B.C. (Ph. M. Giraud-Héraud)
41	Janus head from Roquepertuse. 3rd century B.C. Musée Borély, Marseilles. (Ph. J. J. Hatt)
42	Squatting figure from Roquepertuse. 3rd century B.C. Musée Borély, Marseilles. (Ph. J. J. Hatt)

168   *Funerary portraits of a priestess and a Roman officer. Nîmes. End of 1st century A.D. Nîmes Museum. (Ph. J. J. Hatt)*

169   *Funerary stele from Nickenich. About 40 A.D. Bonn Museum. (Ph. Museum)*

170   *Funerary portrait. Nîmes. End of 1st century A.D. Nîmes Museum. (Ph. J. J. Hatt).*

171   *Funerary portrait. Nîmes. End of 1st century A.D. Nîmes Museum. (Ph. J. J. Hatt)*

172   *Funerary stele of Albinius Asper. Beginning of 2nd century A.D. Trier Museum. (Ph. J. J. Hatt)*

173   *Votive stele of the Mothers of Bonn. End of 2nd century A.D. Bonn Museum. (Ph. Museum)*

174   *Head of a peasant: detail from the Neumagen funerary relief. 2nd century A.D. Trier Museum. (Ph. J. J. Hatt)*

175   *Head of a schoolmaster: detail from the Neumagen funerary relief. 2nd century A.D. Trier Museum. (Ph. J. J. Hatt)*

176   *Farmers paying their rent: detail from the Neumagen funerary relief. 2nd century A.D. Trier Museum. (Ph. J. J. Hatt)*

177   *A schoolmaster and his pupils: detail from the Neumagen funerary relief. 2nd century A.D. Trier Museum. (Ph. J. J. Hatt)*

178   *Detail from the Neumagen boat: the gloomy boatman. End of 2nd century A.D. Trier Museum. (Ph. J. J. Hatt)*

179   *The same: the cheerful boatman.*

180   *Father and son. Arlon. End of 2nd century A.D. Arlon Museum. (Ph. J. J. Hatt)*

181   *Funerary portraits of a family of craftsmen. Saint-Ambroix. 3rd century A.D. Bourges Museum. (Ph. J. J. Hatt)*

182   *Peasants at their meal. Neumagen. 3rd century A.D. Trier Museum. (Ph. J. J. Hatt)*

183   *Head of a Gallo-Roman peasant. 3rd century A.D. Epinal Museum. (Ph. J. J. Hatt)*

184   *Statuette of Hercules holding a lamp. Bronze. 3rd century A.D. Strasbourg. Strasbourg Museum. (Ph. G. Bertin)*

185   *Statuette of a Lar. Strasbourg. Bronze. 1st century A.D. Strasbourg Museum. (Ph. J. J. Hatt)*

186   *Gallic Jupiter. Strasbourg. Bronze. 3rd century A.D. Strasbourg Museum. (Ph. J. J. Hatt)*

187   *Bottle used in the bath, in the form of a Nubian. Strasbourg. Bronze. End of 1st century A.D. Strasbourg Museum. (Ph. J. J. Hatt)*

188   *Bronze appliqué ornament representing the youthful Bacchus. Middle of 1st century A.D. Strasbourg. Strasbourg Museum. (Ph. G. Bertin)*

189   *Statuette of Mercury from Saverne. Bronze. Beginning of 2nd century A.D. Strasbourg Museum. (Ph. J. J. Hatt)*

190   *Statuette of Vulcan. Bronze. Strasbourg. Middle of 1st century A.D· Strasbourg Museum. (Ph. J. J. Hatt)*

191   *Appliqué ornament representing Juno, from Strasbourg. Bronze. 3rd century A.D. Strasbourg Museum. (Ph. J. J. Hatt)*

192   *Votive figurine of Minerva, from Ehl. Bronze. 2nd century A.D. Strasbourg Museum. (Ph. E. Kern)*

193   *Bowl of* terra sigillata, *with relief decoration by Germanus of La Graufesenque depicting a fight between a lion and a wild boar. Middle of 1st century A.D. Strasbourg Museum. (Ph. J. J. Hatt)*

194   *Bowl of* terra sigillata, *with relief decoration by Germanus of La Graufesenque depicting the sacrifice of a victim in front of a tree in which a bird is perched. Middle of 1st century A.D. Strasbourg Museum. (Ph. J. J. Hatt)*

195   *Glass bowl decorated with coloured studs. Strasbourg. 4th century A.D. Strasbourg Museum. (Ph. J. J. Hatt)*

196   *Bowl of engraved glass (filled with wine) depicting a village dance. From the Roman cemetery at Stephansfeld-Brumath. 4th century A.D. Strasbourg Museum. (Ph. G. Bertin)*

197   *Glass bottle and cup from a tomb at Koenigshoffen. End of 3th century A.D. Strasbourg Museum. (Ph. G. Bertin)*

198   *Glass jugs of regional manufacture. From a cemetery at Strasbourg. 4th century A.D. Strasbourg Museum. (Ph. G. Bertin)*

199   *Glass jug. Strasbourg. 4th century A.D. Strasbourg Museum. (Ph. J. J. Hatt)*

200–202 *Cup of engraved crystal (filled with wine) from the Strasbourg cemetery, depicting Abraham's sacrifice and Moses striking the rock. 4th century A.D. Strasbourg Museum. (Ph. G. Bertin)*

323

HALLSTATT AND
LA TÈNE SITES

MOOK
KEMPEN
EYGENBILSEN

SCHWARZENBACH
RODENBAC
AULNAY-AUX-PLANCHES
LES JOGASSES
6   7
SOMME BIONNE
8
10   11
12
POUAN
SENS   VIX
COLMAR
LA COLOMBINE
ALESIA
MÜLHAUSEN
MULHOUSE
BIBRACTE
MERCEY
BOURGES
MANTOCHE
GRÄCHWY
SALINS   LA TÈN
CONLIÈGE
CLERMONT-FERRAND
LYON
VIENNE
MALPAS
CHABESTAN
LE PÈGUE
PERTUIS
PÉZENAS   GLANUM
ENSÉRUNE   ENTREMONT
MAILHAC   MASSILIA
AGDE   SAINT-
BLAISE

6   HATTEN
7   DÜRKHEIM
8   HAGENAU
9   KLEIN ASPERGLEN
10 BRUMATH
11 STRASSBURG STRASBOURG
12 KAPPEL AM RHEIN

AMPURIAS

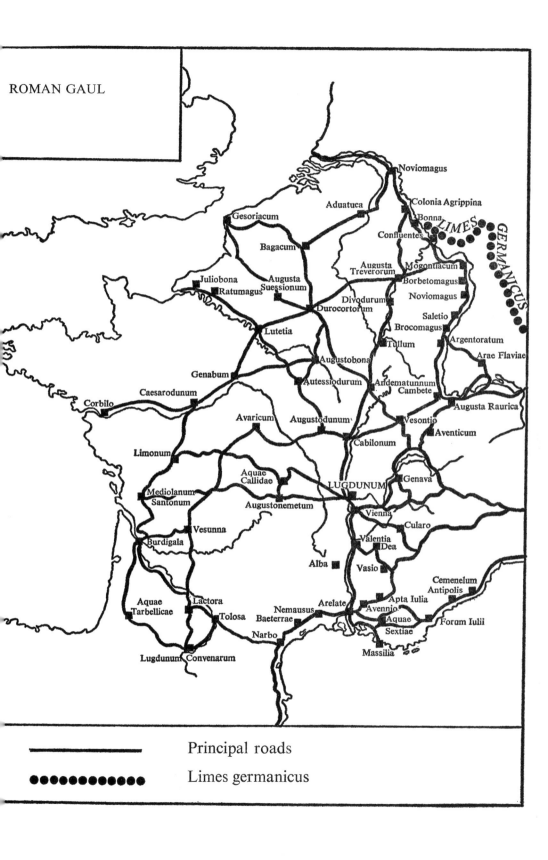

ROMAN GAUL

Noviomagus
Colonia Agrippina
Aduatuca
Gesoriacum
Bonna
LIMES
Bagacum
Confluentes
GERMANICUS
Augusta
Treverorum
Mogontiacum
Juliobona
Augusta
Borbetomagus
Ratumagus
Suessionum
Noviomagus
Divodurum
Saletio
Durocortorum
Brocomagus
Lutetia
Tullum
Argentoratum
Augustobona
Arae Flaviae
Genabum
Autessiodurum
Andematunnum
Caesarodunum
Cambete
Corbilo
Avaricum
Augustodunum
Augusta Raurica
Augustodunum
Vesontio
Cabilonum
Aventicum
Limonum
Aquae
Callidae
LUGDUNUM
Genava
Mediolanum
Santonum
Augustonemetum
Vienna
Vesunna
Culuro
Burdigala
Valentia
Dea
Alba
Vasio
Cemenelum
Antipolis
Aquae
Tarbellicae
Lactora
Arelate
Apta Iulia
Nemausus
Avennio
Tolosa
Baeterrae
Aquae
Forum Iulii
Narbo
Sextiae
Lugdunum Convenarum
Massilia

— Principal roads

•••••••••••••• Limes germanicus

INDEX

(Figures in italics refer to illustrations)

THE TEXT AND ILLUSTRATIONS
IN THIS VOLUME WERE PRINTED
ON THE PRESSES OF
NAGEL PUBLISHERS IN GENEVA

FINISHED IN SEPTEMBER 1970
BINDING BY NAGEL PUBLISHERS,
GENEVA

OFFSET COLOUR SEPARATIONS BY
FOTOLITO ARTISTICA ITALIANA, MILANO

LEGAL DEPOSIT No 513

PRINTED IN SWITZERLAND